EASY DOES IT
WINNERS & FAVORITES

EASY DOES IT
WINNERS & FAVORITES

patty roper

QUAIL RIDGE PRESS

BRANDON, MISSISSIPPI

For my mother Evelyn Slay, my sister Peggy Foggin, my daughter Beth Roper,
and dear friends, Lena Causey and Mary Graves

ISBN–13: 978–1–934193–69–3
ISBN–10: 1-934193-69-0

On the cover: Peaches and Cream Tarts, page 184
Cover design by Bonnie Dickerson
Cover photo by Ron Blaylock
Printed in Canada

First edition, October 2011

Quail Ridge Press
P. O. Box 123 • Brandon, MS 39043
info@quailridge.com • www.quailridge.com

Library of Congress Cataloging-in-Publication Data

Roper, Patty.
    Easy does it : winners & favorites / patty roper.
    p. cm.
    Includes index.
    ISBN–13: 978–1–934193–69–3
    ISBN–10: 1-934193-69-0
1. Cooking, American—Southern style. I. Title.
    TX715.2.S68R67 2011
    641.5975—dc23   2011031748

 Recipe Contest Winner

INTRODUCTION

As southerners, many memories are created around the table sharing food and fellowship with people we love. Traditions are made and kept with family and friends and passed to the next generations through time-tested recipes. Thanksgiving and Christmas would not be the same without sweet potatoes, cranberries, and cornbread dressing prepared from grandmother's recipes. Chocolate and pecan pies and iced layer cakes, prepared by certain family members, always take their place on the sideboard. We look forward to the familiarity of favorite tastes and aromas of special gatherings, just as we cherish our family connections. Our heritage is richly steeped in an association of family, friends, and food.

Easy Does It: Winners and Favorites is a collection of these favorite recipes. Many are winners of recipe contests and were created for special occasions or for special people. The Coconut Pound Cake, a grand-prize recipe contest winner, is a cake that mother and daughter Peggy Shivers and Susan Lott take to friends in times of need. Lime Freeze was created by Joan Ferguson for her niece's bridesmaids' luncheon. Some are recipes shared by accomplished cooks, chefs, and restaurants, and others are quick-and-easy favorites.

So, whether you are preparing a formal dinner with many courses before an extraordinary entrée ending with an over-the-top dessert, or just having girlfriends over for chicken salad with pimiento cheese sandwiches, or looking for cookies and candies for teachers and neighbors, it is all in *Winners and Favorites*—in a truly easy-does-it way with amazing photographs in delightful settings, displaying much more than just great food.

I hope you enjoy planning easy winning and favorite recipes for your family and friends and that *Winners and Favorites* brings much enjoyment to your entertaining.

Patty Roper

ACKNOWLEDGMENTS Thank you to God for guidance and blessings throughout my life and this project; my husband Richard, for being an encouraging sous chef; my mother for love and support; my daughter Beth for love and encouragement; Gwen and Barney McKee for support and development of this project; Cyndi Clark for her artistic design talents and looking at every single picture; Bonnie Dickerson for taking numerous photographs and designing the cover; Terresa Ray for proofreading; Pat Caskey, Lena Causey, Gale Hammond, and Pat Stockett for preparing recipes; Sara McDaniel for recipe testing and organization; photographers Ron Blaylock, Tom Beck, Greg Campbell, and Tempy Segrest for their talents; and the many friends, family members, and recipe contest winners for sharing recipes.

CONTENTS

Okra with Pimiento Cheese and Eggplant Crostini

APPETIZERS

Bacon-Wrapped Figs 12

Bacon-Wrapped Brussels
    Sprouts 12

Eggplant Crostini 13

Prosciutto-Wrapped
    Asparagus 13

Okra with Pimiento Cheese 14

Stuffed Mushrooms 14

Grape Tomato Bites 15

Stuffed New Potatoes 15

Salmon on Puff Pastry 15

Praline Little Smokies 15

Cream Cheese Shells 16

Bacon-Tomato Tartlets 16

Blue Cheese Walnut Tartlets 16

Crabmeat Tartlets 16

Brie and Pepper Jelly
    Tartlets 16

Puff Pastry Breadsticks 19

Barbeque Breadsticks 19

Bacon-Wrapped Breadsticks 19

Cheese and Olive Balls 19

Party Crackers 20

Spicy Crackers 20

Cheese Crackers 20

Fire Crackers 20

Toasted Pecans 21

Spicy Toasted Pecans 21

Gold Leaf Pecans 21

Herb Cheesecake 23

Cheddar Cheesecake 23

Baked Brie 23

Cherry Mice 23

Brie Wedding Cake 24

Brie with a Heart 24

Pumpkin Dip 25

Hospitality Fruit Dip 25

Fantastic Fruit Dip 25

Roasted Red Pepper Hummus 25

Guacamole 25

Cucumber Dip 27

Vegetable Dip 27

Caramelized Onion, Spinach,
    and Artichoke Dip 27

Kozy Shrimp Bake 28

Corn and Avocado Dip 28

Melinda's Hot Turnip Green
    Dip 29

Bacon-Wrapped Figs

BACON-WRAPPED FIGS

This is a beautiful way to enjoy seasonal figs.

6 thin slices bacon
3 ounces goat cheese
1 tablespoon chopped fresh rosemary
12 small ripe figs

Partially cook bacon in microwave for 2 minutes. Blot with paper towels, and cut in half. Mix goat cheese and rosemary together. Slice figs in half lengthwise. Place ½ teaspoon goat cheese mixture between fig halves, and wrap with bacon. Secure with toothpicks. Grill, watching carefully so bacon doesn't flame up, until bacon is crispy. Yield: 12 servings

BACON-WRAPPED BRUSSELS SPROUTS

10 thin slices bacon, cut in half
10 Brussels sprouts, halved lengthwise

Preheat oven to 400 degrees. Partially cook bacon in microwave for 2 minutes. Drain; wrap a bacon piece around each Brussels sprout half; secure with a toothpick. Place sprouts flat side down, on greased wire rack on a baking sheet. Sprinkle with black pepper. Bake 20–25 minutes, until bacon is crisp and Brussels sprouts are tender. Serve with Creamy Mustard Sauce. Yield: 6–8 servings

CREAMY MUSTARD SAUCE:

½ cup sour cream
2 tablespoons whole-grain mustard
1 teaspoon brown sugar
Salt and black pepper to taste

Combine ingredients.

EGGPLANT CROSTINI

1 medium eggplant, peeled and diced
1 teaspoon salt
3 tablespoons chopped fresh basil
1 tablespoon minced garlic
½ cup olive oil
Black pepper to taste
1 small loaf French bread, sliced ¼-inch thick
¾ cup prepared pesto
1 (7-ounce) jar sliced roasted red peppers, drained
1 cup shredded Swiss cheese
¾ cup crumbled feta cheese

Drain eggplant sprinkled with salt for 45 minutes. Preheat oven to 375 degrees. Sauté eggplant, basil, and garlic in olive oil 10 minutes; season with pepper. On each slice of bread, spread 1 teaspoon pesto and 2 teaspoons eggplant. Top with 2 slices roasted pepper. Sprinkle with 2 teaspoons Swiss and 1 teaspoon feta cheese. Bake 20 minutes.
Yield: 16–20 appetizers

PROSCIUTTO-WRAPPED ASPARAGUS

This appetizer is absolutely delicious served as a vegetable.

1 bunch fresh asparagus, trimmed and ends removed
1 slice prosciutto for each stalk
Olive oil
Cracked black pepper

Preheat oven to 325 degrees. Wrap each piece of asparagus with prosciutto. Place on a cookie sheet, drizzle with olive oil, and sprinkle with pepper. Bake for 15 minutes.
Yield: 16 servings

Prosciutto-Wrapped Asparagus

OKRA WITH PIMIENTO CHEESE

A great way to "dress up" pimiento cheese.

1 (16-ounce) jar pickled okra
1½ cups pimiento cheese
1 tablespoon Zatarain's Creole Mustard
Salt, black pepper, and white pepper to taste

Make a lengthwise slice in okra pods and drain on paper towels for 10–15 minutes. Combine pimiento cheese, mustard, salt, and peppers. Stuff each pod with pimiento cheese mixture.
Yield: 20–24 servings

STUFFED MUSHROOMS

These are so easy, and everyone loves them.

1 (8-ounce) package cream cheese, softened
1 (3-ounce) package real bacon bits
1–2 teaspoons garlic powder
30 fresh button mushrooms, stems removed
3 tablespoons butter

Preheat oven to 350 degrees. Mix together cream cheese, bacon bits, and garlic powder, and set aside. Brown mushrooms in butter over medium heat until tender, removing any liquid. Generously stuff mushrooms with cream cheese mixture. Place in pan or baking dish with sides. Bake 20–30 minutes. Serve warm.
Yield: 30 servings

Okra with Pimiento Cheese

GRAPE TOMATO BITES

These are individual Caprese salads.

1 pint grape tomatoes, halved
Fresh mozzarella, cut into ½-inch cubes
4-inch wooden skewers
Balsamic vinaigrette
Fresh basil, chopped
Kosher salt to taste
Black pepper to taste

Skewer 1 tomato half, 1 piece of cheese, and the other tomato half onto each skewer. Place skewers in a shallow serving dish. Drizzle dressing over skewers then sprinkle with basil, salt, and pepper.
Yield: 36 servings

STUFFED NEW POTATOES

20 small, unpeeled new potatoes
1 cup finely chopped, cooked ham
½ cup ricotta cheese
1 (8-ounce) package cream cheese, softened
½ cup mayonnaise
1 teaspoon minced onions
1 tablespoon Dijon mustard
For garnish: paprika and parsley sprigs

Steam potatoes in a vegetable steamer over boiling water for 10 minutes until tender. Cool, and cut potatoes in half. Scoop white pulp from potatoes, and set aside shells. With food processor, pulse potato pulp, ham, ricotta, cream cheese, mayonnaise, onions, and mustard. Pipe ham mixture onto each potato half. Sprinkle with paprika, and garnish with parsley.
Yield: 40 servings

SALMON ON PUFF PASTRY

This appetizer is a favorite at any party.

1½ sheets puff pastry
1 (8-ounce) package cream cheese, softened
2 tablespoons drained and chopped capers
2 tablespoons chopped green onions
½ teaspoon horseradish
1 teaspoon freshly squeezed lemon juice
Salt to taste
8 ounces smoked salmon
For garnish: fresh dill

Preheat oven to 400 degrees. With a 2-inch cookie cutter, cut pastry sheets into 30 rounds. Bake 12 minutes; set aside. Mix together cream cheese, capers, onions, horseradish, lemon juice, and salt. Spread mixture on puff pastry rounds. Cut salmon into 30 pieces and put over cheese mixture. Garnish with dill.
Yield: 30 servings

PRALINE LITTLE SMOKIES

The brown sugar makes these little smokies so sweet.

2 (1-pound) packages little smokies
1 pound bacon
½ cup packed brown sugar

Preheat oven to 350 degrees. Wrap ¼ slice of bacon around each little smokie and secure with a toothpick. Place in baking pan lined with foil and sprinkle with brown sugar. Bake for 20 minutes or until bacon is cooked. Drain and serve.
Yield: 24–36 servings

CREAM CHEESE SHELLS

1 stick butter, softened
1 (3-ounce) package cream cheese, softened
¼ teaspoon salt
1 cup all-purpose flour

Preheat oven to 350 degrees. With mixer, cream butter and cream cheese. Mix in salt and flour. Form into 1-inch balls and press into bottom and up sides of greased mini muffin tins. Bake for 8–10 minutes. Cool and fill with chicken salad, shrimp salad, pimiento cheese, cut-up fruit, or dips.
Yield: 16 tart shells

BACON-TOMATO TARTLETS

These are everyone's favorite appetizer.

1 (10-ounce) can Ro-Tel tomatoes, well drained
1 cup shredded Swiss cheese
1 cup mayonnaise
1 (3-ounce) package real bacon bits
3 (1.9-ounce) packages mini filo shells, thawed

Preheat oven to 350 degrees. Combine tomatoes, cheese, mayonnaise, and bacon bits. Fill shells with 1½ teaspoons mixture and place on baking sheet. Bake 10–15 minutes.
Yield: 45 tartlets

BLUE CHEESE WALNUT TARTLETS

1 (12-ounce) can buttermilk biscuits
1 (3-ounce) package real bacon bits
½ cup crumbled blue cheese
½ cup finely chopped walnuts
1 green onion, chopped
½ cup mayonnaise

Preheat oven to 350 degrees. Split each biscuit into 3 pieces. Press dough into mini muffin tins. Combine bacon, cheese, walnuts, onion, and mayonnaise. Fill shells, and bake 10–12 minutes.
Yield: 30 tartlets

CRABMEAT TARTLETS

1 (6½-ounce) can crabmeat, drained and flaked
2 teaspoons lemon juice
½ cup finely shredded Parmesan cheese
½ cup mayonnaise
2 teaspoons chopped parsley
White pepper and paprika to taste
3 (1.9-ounce) packages mini filo shells, thawed

Preheat oven to 350 degrees. Combine crabmeat, lemon juice, cheese, mayonnaise, parsley, pepper, and paprika. Fill shells with 1½ teaspoons mixture, and place on baking sheet. Bake for 10 minutes until mixture bubbles.
Yield: 45 tartlets

BRIE AND PEPPER JELLY TARTLETS

Also delicious served at room temperature.

1 (12-ounce) can buttermilk biscuits
1 (8-ounce) wheel Brie cheese
2 tablespoons butter
½ cup chopped walnuts, toasted
Cranberry hot pepper jelly or raspberry jam

Preheat oven to 350 degrees. Split each biscuit into 3 pieces. Press dough into mini muffin tins. Cut Brie into 24 (1-inch) cubes; freeze. Sauté walnuts in butter, and set aside. Place one Brie cube in center of each pastry. Bake for 8 minutes. Remove from oven and immediately top each tart with ½ teaspoon of pepper jelly or jam and walnuts.
Yield: 30 tartlets

PUFF PASTRY BREADSTICKS

These breadsticks are so easy and can be prepared in minutes. They can also be used in a tablescape, trailing down a table in tall, stemmed glasses, interspersed with pots of colorful flowers.

1 sheet puff pastry
1 egg, beaten
Fresh herbs
Sesame seeds, poppy seeds
Parmesan cheese, grated
Asparagus spears

Preheat oven to 400 degrees. Brush one sheet puff pastry with egg. Sprinkle with herbs, spices, or Parmesan cheese. Cut into ¾-inch strips, and twist, and place on lightly greased baking sheet. Or wrap puff pastry strips, brushed with egg, around each asparagus spear, and place on greased baking sheet. Bake for 10–15 minutes.
Yield: 12 sticks per sheet of puff pastry

BARBEQUE BREADSTICKS

1½ cups coarsely grated extra sharp Cheddar cheese
1 cup all-purpose flour, plus more for dusting
¾ stick unsalted butter, cut into tablespoons
½ teaspoon salt
1 tablespoon barbeque seasoning
2 tablespoons heavy cream

Preheat oven to 350 degrees. In food processor, combine cheese, flour, butter, salt, and barbeque seasoning; pulse several times. Add cream, and pulse to form a ball. Roll out ½ inch thick on floured surface. Cut into one-inch strips. Place on parchment-lined baking sheets, and bake for 15 minutes, rotating once. Cool on pans.
Yield: 36 breadsticks

BACON-WRAPPED BREADSTICKS

Men and children love these breadsticks, so make plenty. They are also great for brunches.

1 cup packed dark brown sugar
1 tablespoon chili seasoning mix
2 pounds thin-sliced bacon
40–50 Grissini Breadsticks

Spread brown sugar on tray, and dry for one hour. Add chili seasoning mix. Preheat oven to 300 degrees. Dip bacon slices in sugar mixture; coating both sides well. Spiral-wrap coated bacon around bread stick. Place on a cookie sheet lined with greased foil. Bake for 30–40 minutes until bacon is cooked. Breadsticks will be soft but will harden.
Yield: 40–50 breadsticks

CHEESE AND OLIVE BALLS

½ pound sharp Cheddar cheese, finely shredded
1 stick butter, softened
2 cups all-purpose flour
½ teaspoon salt
½ teaspoon ground red pepper
1 teaspoon paprika
36 pimiento-stuffed olives

Preheat oven to 400 degrees. Mix together all ingredients except olives. Wrap a small piece of dough around each olive. Place on greased baking sheet. Bake for 10–12 minutes or until lightly browned.
Yield: 36 appetizers

PARTY CRACKERS

This is a simple way to make ordinary crackers special.

Crackers
Butter
Onion salt
Grated Parmesan cheese
Worcestershire sauce

Preheat oven to 350 degrees. Brush crackers with butter and sprinkle with onion salt, Parmesan cheese, and Worcestershire sauce. Bake on a greased cookie sheet 10–15 minutes.

SPICY CRACKERS

These crackers are sought-after gifts at Christmas.

6 boxes of your favorite crackers (Sociables, Chicken in a Biscuit, Ritz or Ritz Sticks, Cheese Nips, Wheat Thins, Mini Club Crackers)
4 tablespoons Worcestershire sauce
¾ cup vegetable oil
1½ sticks butter, melted
3 tablespoons Ac'cent
2 teaspoons crushed red pepper flakes
3 teaspoons garlic salt
3 teaspoons chili powder
3 tablespoons Tabasco sauce

Preheat oven to 250 degrees. Empty all crackers into a medium garbage bag and mix well. Whisk other ingredients together and pour into bag over crackers. Mix carefully to avoid breaking crackers. Place crackers on 3 large baking sheets and bake for 30 minutes, stirring occasionally.
Yield: 6 boxes spicy crackers

CHEESE CRACKERS

These are great cut into shapes with small cookie cutters.

8 ounces sharp Cheddar cheese, grated and softened
1 stick butter, softened
½ teaspoon salt
1¼ teaspoons cayenne pepper
1½ cups all-purpose flour

Preheat oven to 350 degrees. Cream cheese and butter; add seasonings. Add 1½ cups flour to form stiff dough. Roll out ½ inch thick on floured surface. Cut into shapes with a small cookie cutter, or press through a cookie press with a star tip. Place on a greased cookie sheet, and bake for 25 minutes or until lightly browned.
Yield: about 5 dozen

FIRE CRACKERS

These crackers are perfect to serve with soups and salads.

½ cup canola oil
3 tablespoons crushed red pepper flakes
1 (1-ounce) package dry ranch dressing mix
3 stacks saltine crackers or Town House Crackers

Combine oil, red pepper, and ranch dressing. Pour oil mixture over crackers, one stack at a time, until all is used. Place crackers in a container with a lid. Turn container every 15 minutes for one hour. Store in an airtight container.
Yield: 24 servings

TOASTED PECANS

1 stick butter
4 cups pecan halves
1 teaspoon salt

Preheat oven to 400 degrees. Melt butter in 9x13-inch pan. Stir in pecans and salt. Place in 400-degree oven; then turn oven off. Leave for 15 minutes without opening door.
Yield: 4 cups

SPICY TOASTED PECANS

3 cups pecan halves
2 tablespoons margarine, melted
½ teaspoon each: cumin, cayenne pepper, thyme, grated nutmeg, and black pepper
1 teaspoon salt

Preheat oven to 350 degrees. In bowl, toss all ingredients together. Spread on ungreased, foil-lined baking sheet, and bake for 15 minutes, stirring every 5 minutes.
Yield: 3 cups

GOLD LEAF PECANS

These are the ultimate treat!

¾ cup sugar
1 teaspoon cinnamon
½ teaspoon salt
¼ teaspoon each: nutmeg, allspice, and cloves
1 egg white
2½ teaspoons water
8 cups pecan halves
¾ teaspoon edible gold leaf

Preheat oven to 275 degrees. Combine sugar, spices, egg white, and water in a zipper bag. Add pecans, and coat well. Spread on lightly greased, foil-lined cookie sheet. Sprinkle with gold leaf. Bake for 50–55 minutes. Stir occasionally. Remove and cool on wax paper.
Yield: 8 cups

Gold
Leaf
Pecans

HERB CHEESECAKE

This cheesecake is a special blend of herbs.

1 cup plus 3 tablespoons all-purpose flour, divided
½ cup butter
1 egg yolk
2 teaspoons lemon zest
3 (8-ounce) packages cream cheese
¾ cup grated or shredded Parmesan cheese
1 onion, finely chopped
⅔ cup chopped parsley
2 teaspoons salt
4 eggs
½ teaspoon Tabasco sauce
2 tablespoons lemon juice
1 teaspoon each oregano, tarragon, basil, and
    rosemary

For crust, in food processor, blend 1 cup flour, butter, yolk, and zest to crumb consistency. Press into bottom and up sides of 8-inch spring-form pan; freeze. Preheat oven to 400 degrees. In processor, combine cream cheese, Parmesan, onion, and parsley until smooth. Add remaining 3 tablespoons flour, salt, and eggs. Blend in Tabasco, lemon juice, and herbs. Pour into crust. Bake 10 minutes, reduce heat to 325 degrees, and bake 50 minutes. Cool 1 hour before serving with crackers.
Yield: 48 servings

CHEDDAR CHEESECAKE

2 pounds shredded Cheddar cheese, softened
1 bunch green onions, chopped
1 pound bacon, cooked and crumbled
2 tablespoons mayonnaise
For garnish: apricot preserves, raspberries, slivered
    almonds, and green onions

Mix all ingredients together; pour into a greased 9-inch springform pan. Chill. Garnish top with preserves, raspberries, almonds, and green onions. Serve with crackers.
Yield: 30–36 servings

BAKED BRIE

This beautiful appetizer is very easy to prepare.

1 sheet puff pastry
1 (15-ounce) wheel Brie cheese, with rind
½ cup raspberry jam
2 tablespoons maple syrup
2 tablespoons brown sugar
½ cup chopped pecans, toasted
1 egg, beaten

Preheat oven to 350 degrees. Place half of puff pastry sheet on a greased cookie sheet. Place Brie in center of puff pastry, and trim to fit; reserve trimmings. Spread top of Brie with jam. Drizzle with maple syrup, brown sugar, and pecans. Cover with remaining half sheet of puff pastry, tucking ends under. Make a small bow with puff pastry strip from trimmings, and place on top. Brush surface and bow with beaten egg, and bake for 25–30 minutes. Serve with crackers and apple slices.
Yield: 24 servings

CHERRY MICE

These mice are adorable sitting on a cheese tray.

12 fresh cherries with stems
2 ounces chocolate almond bark, melted
24 almond slices
12 mini chocolate chips
Blue and red piping gel

Dip each cherry with a stem in melted chocolate. Add 2 sliced almonds for ears and a small chocolate chip as a nose. Place on wax paper to harden. When hardened, pipe on eyes with blue icing dots and a nose on the chocolate chip with a red icing dot.

Brie Wedding Cake

BRIE WEDDING CAKE

This is such a special presentation for a wedding party.

1 (10-ounce) wheel Brie cheese, with rind
1 (8-ounce) wheel Brie cheese, with rind
1 (5-ounce) wheel Brie cheese, with rind
2 (8-ounce) containers whipped cream cheese
For garnish: fresh berries

Stack Bries from larger to smaller. Ice with cream cheese. Pipe flowers on Brie with cream cheese in a pastry bag with star tip. Garnish with berries. Serve with crackers.
Yield: 24–36 servings

BRIE WITH A HEART

Cut any shape for any occasion.

1 (8-ounce) wheel Brie cheese, with rind
½ cup strawberry jam
For garnish: fresh mint and strawberries

Carefully slice top rind off Brie, and reserve. Spread Brie with jam. Cut a heart or chosen shape from reserved top rind and replace over jam. Serve with crackers.
Yield: 12–16 servings

PUMPKIN DIP

Serve this dip from a small pumpkin.

2 (8-ounce) packages cream cheese, softened
4 cups confectioners' sugar
3 teaspoons cinnamon
2 teaspoons vanilla
1 (15-ounce) can pumpkin pie filling
½ teaspoon ground ginger
½ teaspoon nutmeg

Beat cream cheese and sugar. Add remaining ingredients. Chill. Serve with ginger snaps.
Yield: 8 cups

HOSPITALITY FRUIT DIP

This dip is such a special surprise.

1 (8-ounce) package cream cheese, softened
1⅓ cups sugar
⅓ cup half-and-half
3 tablespoons vanilla
1 teaspoon nutmeg

Pulse ingredients in food processor until smooth. Chill before serving. Serve with fresh, seasonal fruit.
Yield: 3 cups

FANTASTIC FRUIT DIP

1 (8-ounce) package cream cheese, softened
2 tablespoons butter, softened
¾ cup confectioners' sugar, sifted
2 tablespoons orange juice
1 tablespoon grated orange rind
1 teaspoon vanilla

Combine all ingredients, and chill at least 30 minutes before serving. Great with apples or any firm fruit.
Yield: 2 cups

ROASTED RED PEPPER HUMMUS

1 (15-ounce) can navy beans, rinsed and drained
3 garlic cloves, chopped
¾ cup roasted red bell peppers, drained
⅓ cup tahini
¼ cup fresh lemon juice
½ teaspoon ground cumin
¼ teaspoon ground red pepper
2 tablespoons olive oil
1 tablespoon chopped cilantro
For garnish: toasted sesame seeds

In food processor, pulse beans, garlic, bell peppers, tahini, lemon juice, cumin, and red pepper until smooth. With processor running, pour oil through food chute in a slow, steady stream, and process until smooth. Stir in cilantro. Garnish with toasted sesame seeds. Serve with pita chips.
Yield: 2 cups

GUACAMOLE

This is everyone's favorite recipe from Babalu, a restaurant in Jackson, Mississippi.

2 large avocados, halved and pitted
1 tablespoon thinly sliced green onion
1½ tablespoons finely minced red onion
1½ tablespoons freshly squeezed lime juice
1 tablespoon finely chopped cilantro
1½ tablespoons chopped sun-dried tomatoes
½ teaspoon salt

Remove meat from avocados. Add onions, lime juice, cilantro, and tomatoes. Sprinkle salt over all ingredients to evenly incorporate. Mash with a potato masher, keeping mixture somewhat chunky, and serve with freshly fried corn tortilla chips.
Yield: 4 servings

Vegetable Dip

CUCUMBER DIP

1 large seedless cucumber, peeled and chopped
½ teaspoon salt
2 tablespoons sour cream
1 (8-ounce) package cream cheese, softened
1 teaspoon lemon juice
1 teaspoon chopped thyme
1 teaspoon lemon zest
Black and white pepper to taste
For garnish: fresh thyme

In a food processor, purée cucumber with salt, and set aside. With a mixer, cream sour cream, cream cheese, and lemon juice. Stir in thyme, zest, and peppers. Stir in puréed cucumber, and chill. Garnish with thyme, and serve with fresh, raw vegetables.
Yield: 1½ cups

VEGETABLE DIP

1 (8-ounce) package cream cheese, softened
2 tablespoons milk
2 tablespoons grated Parmesan cheese
4 tablespoons ranch salad dressing mix
¼ cup chopped red bell pepper
1 green onion, chopped

With mixer, beat cream cheese and milk at medium speed until creamy. Add cheese and dressing mix. Stir in bell pepper and green onion. Chill. Serve in vegetable containers with assorted fresh, raw vegetables.
Yield: 2 cups

CARAMELIZED ONION, SPINACH, AND ARTICHOKE DIP

Everyone enjoys this combination.

2 Vidalia onions, chopped
1 stick unsalted butter
2 (10-ounce) packages frozen chopped spinach, thawed and drained
1 (12-ounce) jar marinated quartered artichoke hearts, drained and chopped
4 ounces cream cheese, softened
1 cup sour cream
1 cup mayonnaise
¼ cup heavy cream
6 cloves garlic, peeled and chopped
1 teaspoon black pepper
1 tablespoon lemon pepper
1 teaspoon crushed red pepper flakes
2 teaspoons hot pepper sauce
1 tablespoon lemon juice
2 cups grated Parmesan cheese

In a heavy skillet over medium heat, caramelize onions in butter; set aside and cool. In a colander, press spinach to drain liquid. Squeeze drained spinach tightly in small handfuls until almost dry. Add to onions. Stir in artichokes. In food processor, blend cream cheese, sour cream, mayonnaise, cream, garlic, peppers, pepper sauce, and lemon juice. Add Parmesan cheese and pulse a couple of times. Mixture should have a coarse texture. Fold into vegetable mixture. Serve at room temperature or heat in a 350-degree oven until bubbly and slightly brown. Serve with crackers.
Yield: 20–24 servings

Kozy Shrimp Bake

 KOZY SHRIMP BAKE

2 pounds shrimp, peeled and deveined
1 (16-ounce) package smoked sausage, sliced
1 each: bell pepper, onion, and tomato, sliced

SAUCE:
½ cup each: butter and olive oil
¼ cup each: chili sauce and Worcestershire sauce
4 cloves garlic, minced
2 tablespoons Creole seasoning
2 tablespoons lemon juice
*1 teaspoon each: paprika, oregano, red pepper,
    black pepper, and hot sauce*

Spread shrimp and sausage in baking dish. In saucepan, combine Sauce ingredients, stirring until butter melts; pour over shrimp and sausage. Add bell pepper, onion, and tomato; cover with foil. Chill for 2 hours. Preheat oven to 400 degrees. Bake uncovered for 20 minutes. Serve with garlic bread.
Yield: 8 servings

CORN AND AVOCADO DIP

This is a cool, refreshing summertime dip.

5 ears corn
½ stick butter
4 avocados, pitted and cut into small pieces
½ medium red onion, finely chopped
½ bunch cilantro, chopped
½ cup mayonnaise
Black pepper to taste
1 jalapeño, seeded and chopped
Juice of 1½ limes
1 red bell pepper, finely chopped
2 cloves garlic, chopped

Cut kernels from corn, and fry in butter for 5 minutes or until tender; set aside. Combine remaining ingredients. Add corn. Chill. Serve over ice with chips.
Yield: 20–24 servings

MELINDA'S HOT TURNIP GREEN DIP

This dip is so southern served with mini cornbread waffles.

½ medium sweet onion, chopped
2 garlic cloves, chopped
2 tablespoons olive oil
¼ cup dry white wine
1 (14½-ounce) can chopped turnip greens, drained
12 ounces cream cheese, cut into pieces
1 (8-ounce) carton sour cream
½ teaspoon crushed red pepper flakes
¼ teaspoon salt
Sugar to taste
¾ cup freshly grated Parmesan cheese, divided
1 (3-ounce) package real bacon bits

Preheat oven to 350 degrees. Sauté onion and garlic in olive oil. Add wine, and cook for 1–2 minutes. Stir in turnip greens, cream cheese, sour cream, red pepper, salt, sugar, and ½ cup Parmesan cheese. Cook, stirring often, for 6–8 minutes or until cream cheese is melted and mixture is heated. Transfer to a 1½-quart baking dish and top with remaining Parmesan cheese; bake for 10–15 minutes. Sprinkle with bacon. Serve with cornbread waffles.
Yield: 20–24 servings

For cornbread waffles, use your favorite cornbread batter and bake in a greased mini waffle iron.

Melinda's Hot Turnip Green Dip

Pink Lemonade Spritzer

BEVERAGES

Southern Sweet Tea 32

Mint Tea 32

Tea Punch 32

Fruit Tea 32

Apricot Nectar Tea 32

Slushy Fruit Punch 34

Mock Champagne 34

Mock Mint Juleps 35

Golden Punch 35

Cinnamon Apple Cider 35

Berry Spritzer 37

Meyer Lemonade 37

Raspberry Lemonade 37

Pink Lemonade Spritzer 37

Eggnog 38

Coffee Punch 38

Fudge Punch 38

SOUTHERN SWEET TEA

This is the old favorite, made with sugar dissolved in warm tea. Southern people love sweet tea.

8 cups water, divided
2 family-size tea bags
2 cups sugar
For garnish: fresh mint and lemon slices

Bring 4 cups water to a rolling boil. Remove from heat, add tea bags, cover, and steep 30 minutes. Add sugar and stir until dissolved. Add remaining water and chill. Serve over ice with mint and lemon slices.
Yield: 1 gallon

MINT TEA

This is a refreshing low-calorie tea.

3 cups water
12 regular-size mint tea bags
1 (½-ounce) tub lemonade mix
14 packets sugar substitute
For garnish: fresh mint and lemon slices

Bring 3 cups water to a boil. Remove from heat; add tea bags, lemonade, and sugar substitute. Let stand 30 minutes; add water to make 1 gallon, and chill. Serve with mint and lemon slices.
Yield: 1 gallon

TEA PUNCH

This punch may also be served at the table in glasses for a special luncheon or dinner.

1 gallon sweet tea
1 gallon orange juice
1 (46-ounce) can unsweetened pineapple juice
1 gallon lemonade
1 (2-liter) ginger ale
For garnish: orange slices and fresh mint

Mix tea, juices, and lemonade in a glass container, and chill. Add ginger ale just before serving. Garnish with orange slices and mint.
Yield: 4½ gallons

FRUIT TEA

Ladies love this tea for brunches and luncheons.

2 cups water
2 cups sugar
8 regular-size tea bags
2 cups orange juice
1 cup lemon juice
For garnish: fresh mint and lemon and orange slices

Simmer water and sugar for 10 minutes. Remove from heat. Add tea bags. Let stand for at least 20 minutes. To a gallon jug, add tea mixture, orange juice, and lemon juice. Fill with water to make 1 gallon. Garnish with mint and lemon and orange slices.
Yield: 1 gallon

APRICOT NECTAR TEA

So special and sweet, this tea is absolutely delicious!

6 family-size tea bags
2 sprigs mint
1 cup sugar
1 (12-ounce) can frozen lemonade, thawed
4 (11½-ounce) cans apricot nectar
1 teaspoon almond extract
For garnish: fresh mint

Place tea bags, mint, and 2 cups cold water in gallon container. Bring 3 cups water to boil and pour over tea bags. Cover and steep 15 minutes. Remove tea bags and mint. Stir in sugar. Add remaining ingredients and fill with additional water, if necessary, to make 1 gallon. Chill and garnish with mint.
Yield: 1 gallon

Southern Sweet Tea

Mock Champagne

SLUSHY FRUIT PUNCH

This delicious, economical punch can be made ahead.

2 (6-ounce) packages cherry Kool-Aid
2 (6-ounce) packages raspberry Kool-Aid
2 cups sugar
1 (46-ounce) can unsweetened pineapple juice
1 (2-liter) bottle 7-Up

Combine Kool-Aids, sugar, and pineapple juice. Add water to fill a 1-gallon container. Pour into a larger container and place in freezer. Stir when ice crystals form. Stir several more times during freezing, to form a "slushy" consistency. Remove from freezer to refrigerator 2 hours before serving. Add 7-Up just before serving.
Yield: 1 gallon

MOCK CHAMPAGNE

This refreshing, sparkling drink is perfect for celebrations.

2 (32-ounce) bottles white grape juice
1 (64-ounce) bottle apple juice
1 (2-liter) bottle 7-Up

Chill ingredients. Combine white grape juice and apple juice. Place in punch bowl. Add 7-Up just before serving.
Yield: 2 gallons

MOCK MINT JULEPS

Great with appetizers on the porch!

2 cups cold tea
¾ cup sugar
Juice of 2 lemons
Juice of 2 oranges
2 cups white grape juice
2 tablespoons crushed pineapple in juice
1 quart carbonated water
*For garnish: fresh orange wedges, fresh mint, and
    fresh pansies*

Combine tea and sugar, and chill. When ready
to serve, add lemon juice, orange juice, white
grape juice, and crushed pineapple in juice. Pour
into glasses half filled with crushed ice, and top
with orange wedges, mint, and pansies.
Yield: 8 servings

GOLDEN PUNCH

This fruit drink is perfect for breakfast or brunch.

*4 cups each: orange juice, unsweetened pineapple
    juice, white grape juice and ginger ale*
Combine juices; chill. Add ginger ale just before
serving.
Yield: 1 gallon

CINNAMON APPLE CIDER

This is so easy and delicious and is the most
beautiful cherry color.

2 tablespoons cinnamon Red Hots
1 gallon apple cider

Heat Red Hots in apple cider until melted.
Yield: 1 gallon

Mock Mint Juleps

Berry Spritzer

BERRY SPRITZER

This easy-to-prepare spritzer is so light.

1 (2-liter) bottle 7-Up (not diet)
2 regular-size raspberry or berry zinger tea bags
For garnish: fresh berries and fresh mint

Pour ¼ cup of 7-Up from bottle. Add tea bags to bottle of remaining drink. Chill overnight. Serve over crushed ice with fresh berries and mint.
Yield: 12 small servings

MEYER LEMONADE

Meyer lemons have a sweeter taste than regular lemons. This recipe may also be made with lemons or limes.

1 cup sugar
1 cup water
1½ cups Meyer lemon juice (6 lemons)
4 cups cold water
¼ cup fresh mint leaves
1 liter ginger ale
For garnish: fresh mint and lemon slices

Make a simple syrup by heating sugar and water in small saucepan until sugar is dissolved. Cool and add juice. Add cold water and mint leaves. Chill, and serve with ice and sliced lemons. Top each glass with 2 tablespoons of ginger ale just before serving. Garnish with mint and lemon slices.
Yield: 1 gallon

RASPBERRY LEMONADE

Add a raspberry taste and a pink color to lemonade.

1 (10-ounce) package frozen raspberries, thawed
1 (12-ounce) container frozen lemonade, thawed
4 cups water
1 liter ginger ale
For garnish: fresh raspberries, mint, and lemon slices

Process raspberries in food processor, and strain. Combine raspberry juice, lemonade, and water; chill. Pour in ginger ale just before serving. Garnish with raspberries, mint, and lemon slices.
Yield: 1 gallon

PINK LEMONADE SPRITZER

This easy spritzer is so refreshing.

1 gallon water
4 (½-ounce) pink lemonade mix tubs
1 liter ginger ale
For garnish: lemon slices, fresh mint, and maraschino cherries with stems, drained

Combine lemonade mix with water, and chill. Add ginger ale just before serving. Garnish with lemon slices, mint, and cherries.
Yield: 1½ gallons

EGGNOG

A seasonal treat that everyone loves.

6 eggs
1 cup sugar
1 cup milk
2 cups heavy cream
1 tablespoon vanilla
½ teaspoon rum extract
¼ teaspoon nutmeg
For garnish: grated nutmeg

In top of double boiler, beat eggs and sugar. Add milk. Heat and stir until mixture coats spoon. Chill. With mixer, beat cream until soft peaks form. Add vanilla, rum extract, and nutmeg; beat another 2 minutes. Fold cream mixture into egg mixture and pour into serving bowl. Chill. To serve, ladle mixture into cups and sprinkle with nutmeg.
Yield: 6–8 servings

COFFEE PUNCH

A very decadent treat with desserts.

4 cups hot strong coffee
½ cup sugar
1 quart milk
2 pints half-and-half
1 teaspoon vanilla
½ teaspoon almond extract
1 gallon coffee ice cream, softened
1 gallon vanilla ice cream, softened
1 pint heavy cream, whipped
For garnish: maraschino cherries with stems
    and mint

Dissolve sugar in coffee. Stir in milk, half-and-half, vanilla, and almond extract. Pour over ice creams. Cover with whipped cream. Garnish with cherries and mint.
Yield: about 40 cups

FUDGE PUNCH

½ gallon milk
1½ cups chocolate syrup
½ gallon ice cream (vanilla, chocolate, or coffee),
    softened
1 (8-ounce) container whipped topping
For garnish: chocolate shavings and toasted
    almonds

Stir together milk, syrup, and ice cream. Top with whipped topping, chocolate shavings, and almonds.
Yield: 1½ gallons

Coffee Punch

Spicy Pumpkin Soup

SOUPS

SPICY PUMPKIN SOUP

This soup has just the perfect blend of spices.

½ stick butter

3 cloves garlic, minced

2 stalks celery, finely chopped

1 large onion, finely chopped

2 cups chicken broth, divided

2 carrots, finely chopped

1 large potato, finely chopped

1 (15-ounce) can pumpkin

½ cup finely chopped cilantro

½ cup honey

½ cup sugar

2 teaspoons allspice, divided

2 teaspoons cinnamon, divided

2 teaspoons cloves, divided

½ teaspoon crushed red pepper flakes, divided

2 (14-ounce) cans unsweetened coconut milk

Half-and-half

Black pepper to taste

For garnish: half-and-half and cilantro

Melt butter in heavy stockpot. Stir in garlic, celery, and onion. Add ½ cup chicken broth and cook 5 minutes over medium-high heat. Add carrots, potato, and pumpkin, and mix well. Add remaining chicken broth, and bring to a low boil. Add cilantro, honey, sugar, and half of the spices. Stir well and reduce to a simmer. Simmer until potatoes and carrots are tender, stirring often. When vegetables are tender, remove from heat and allow mixture to cool; transfer in batches to blender. Blend until smooth. Return to stockpot and add coconut milk. Add additional spices to taste. Let simmer 15–20 minutes, stirring often. Add half-and-half as needed for desired consistency. Sprinkle with half-and-half, black pepper, and cilantro.
Yield: 12 servings

CREAM OF ASPARAGUS SOUP

2 (16-ounce) cans asparagus, with juice reserved

2½ cups chicken stock, divided

1 cup heavy cream

4 tablespoons butter

4 tablespoons flour

Salt, white pepper, and lemon juice to taste

Drain asparagus, reserving juice. Add stock to juice to make 1 cup; add remaining 2 cups stock, then cream. Cut tips off asparagus; set tips and stems aside. In a heavy saucepan, melt butter, and blend in flour. Cook over medium heat for 3 minutes. Add juice mixture, and continue cooking over medium heat, stirring until mixture thickens. Purée asparagus stems, and add to soup. Season with salt and white pepper and drops of lemon juice. Add reserved asparagus tips, and reheat gently.
Yield: 6 cups

SANTA FE SOUP

1 onion, chopped

2 tablespoons margarine

8 chicken breasts, boiled and cut into chunks

½ cup chicken broth

3 (1-ounce) packages dry ranch dressing mix

3 (1¼-ounce) packages taco seasoning mix

2 (16-ounce) cans black beans

2 (16-ounce) cans kidney beans

2 (16-ounce) cans pinto beans

2 (14½-ounce) cans Ro-Tel tomatoes

2 (14½-ounce) cans tomato wedges

2 (15-ounce) cans white corn

3 cups water

For garnish: sour cream, cheese, and green onions

Sauté chopped onion in margarine. Add chicken and broth. Stir dressing and taco mixes into chicken mixture. Add remaining ingredients with juices. Add water. Simmer for 2 hours. Garnish with sour cream, cheese, and green onions. Serve with tortilla chips or French bread.
Yield: 16–20 servings

Cream of Asparagus Soup

Chicken Vegetable Soup

CHICKEN VEGETABLE SOUP

3 large chicken breasts, with bones and skin
2 (14½-ounce) cans chopped tomatoes, liquid
    included
2 (14½-ounce) cans white corn, drained
1 (10-ounce) package frozen petite butter beans,
    cooked and drained
2 (10¾-ounce) cans alphabet vegetable soup
1 (8-ounce) can tomato sauce
1 soup can water
1 tablespoon celery seeds
2 tablespoons margarine
Salt, black pepper, and sugar to taste

In 4-quart saucepan, boil chicken until tender
in just enough water to cover. Remove bones
and skin, and cut chicken into small pieces; set
aside. To broth, add tomatoes and cook 10 minutes. Add corn, butter beans, chicken, soup, tomato sauce, water, celery seeds, margarine, salt,
pepper, and sugar. Simmer for 20 minutes. Add
more water, if needed. Serve with cornbread.
Yield: 8–12 servings

VEGETABLE BEEF SOUP

2 pounds beef stew meat
Salt and black pepper to taste
6–8 cups water, divided
2 (16-ounce) bags frozen sweet vegetables with
    tomatoes for soup mix
1 (46-ounce) can tomato juice
1 (14½-ounce) can diced tomatoes

Season beef with salt and pepper, and set aside.
In a large saucepan, bring 6 cups water to a
boil. Add beef and bring back to a boil; reduce heat, and simmer for 10–15 minutes until
meat is brown. Turn off heat, and cool to room
temperature. Transfer beef and broth to a large
crockpot. Add vegetables, juice, and diced tomatoes. Heat on LOW for 6 hours. Add additional
water if too thick. Salt and pepper to taste.
Yield: 12–16 servings

FRESH TOMATO SOUP WITH CORNBREAD CROUTONS

½ cup each: finely chopped onion, celery, and
    carrots
1 tablespoon olive oil
Salt and black pepper to taste
4 cups chopped fresh tomatoes
4 cups chicken broth
1 tablespoon minced basil
2 teaspoons sugar
1 teaspoon lemon juice
1 cup half-and-half
2 tablespoons all-purpose flour
2 tablespoons butter
For garnish: grated cheese and chopped green
    onions

In 4-quart saucepan, sauté finely chopped vegetables in olive oil until transparent. Add salt and
pepper. Stir in tomatoes, chicken broth, basil,
sugar, and lemon juice. Bring to a boil, cover,
and simmer for one hour. Blend half-and-half
and flour, and add to soup. Bring back to a full
boil for 5 minutes, and add butter. Ladle soup
into bowls, and top with Cornbread Croutons.
For additional flavor, garnish with grated cheese
and chopped green onions.
Yield: 4–6 servings

CORNBREAD CROUTONS:
Cornbread, diced
2 tablespoons olive oil
1 tablespoon minced basil
Black pepper to taste

Preheat oven to 350 degrees. Brush cornbread
with mixture of olive oil, basil, and pepper. Bake
20 minutes.

SUPERIOR CHILI

3½–4 pounds ground beef, coarsely ground
4 cups beef broth
Olive oil
1 large yellow onion, chopped
1 green bell pepper, chopped
Garlic, minced
Jalapeño, diced
1 (14-ounce) can petite diced tomatoes
3 (15-ounce) cans seasoned diced tomato sauce
    for chili
4 (16-ounce) cans Blue Runner Creole Cream Style
    Red Beans
½ tablespoon salt
Black pepper to taste
1 tablespoon Emeril's Southwest Essence Seasoning
1 teaspoon cumin
4 tablespoons chili powder
1 tablespoon Worcestershire sauce
Generous dash of Crystal hot sauce

Tortilla chips or hot tamales
For garnish: sour cream, grated Cheddar cheese,
    black olives, and chopped onion

In a large skillet, brown beef, drain, and set
aside, reserving drippings. To drippings, add
water and simmer to make 4 cups broth; set
aside. In large pot, sauté onion and bell pepper
in olive oil until softened. Add chopped garlic
and jalapeño, and continue cooking for 3–5 minutes. Add tomatoes, tomato sauce, and beans.
Add salt, pepper, Essence, cumin, chili powder,
Worcestershire, and hot sauce. Mix thoroughly.
Add ground beef and broth. Simmer for 1½
hours. Serve over tortilla chips or hot tamales,
and garnish with sour cream, grated cheese,
black olives, and chopped onion with hot cornbread or tortilla chips.
Yield: 10–12 servings

GUMBO

1 pound andouille sausage, sliced into ⅛-inch
   rounds
¼ cup olive oil
1 cup all-purpose flour
2 large onions, coarsely chopped
2 green bell peppers, coarsely chopped
1 medium head celery, coarsely chopped
1 clove garlic, minced
1 rotisserie chicken, cut into large, bite-size pieces
8 cups chicken broth
1 tablespoon salt
2 teaspoons black pepper
½ teaspoon cayenne pepper
1 teaspoon paprika
1 tablespoon dried thyme
4 bay leaves
1 teaspoon dried oregano
½ teaspoon dried sage
2 tablespoons Worcestershire sauce
2 tablespoons hot sauce
2 pounds medium shrimp, peeled and deveined

In a 10-quart stockpot over medium-high heat, brown sausage. Remove sausage from pan, and add olive oil. When oil is hot, gradually add flour, whisking continuously. Continue to whisk roux (to keep from burning) for about 20 minutes, until roux is dark mahogany in color. Add chopped onions to roux, and continue stirring for 2 minutes. (Onions will sizzle when they hit the hot roux.) Stir in bell peppers, stirring for 2 minutes. Add celery and garlic, and continue stirring 2 minutes. Add chicken, sausage, and broth, and stir well. Add salt, peppers, paprika, thyme, bay leaves, oregano, sage, Worcestershire sauce, and hot sauce. Stir well. Bring gumbo to a boil, and continue boiling for 5 minutes. Reduce heat to maintain a slow simmer, uncovered, for at least an hour and up to 6 hours. If gumbo is too thick, add a little water; if too thin, continue to simmer, uncovered. Add shrimp, and simmer for 5 minutes or until shrimp turn pink. Serve over cooked rice with French bread.
Yield: 24 servings

Cheese Soup

CHEESE SOUP

1 bunch green onions, chopped (including small
   white bulb)
1 stalk celery, chopped
3 tablespoons margarine
2 tablespoons all-purpose flour
1 (10¾-ounce) can cream of chicken soup
2 (15-ounce) cans chicken broth
Dash of Tabasco sauce
1 pound Velveeta cheese, cut into pieces
3 cups shredded Cheddar cheese
2 cups milk
Salt, black pepper, and white pepper to taste

In a large saucepan over medium heat, sauté onions and celery in margarine until tender. Stir in
flour. Add soup, chicken broth, and Tabasco. Stir
in Velveeta until melted. Add shredded Cheddar,
and stir until combined. Add milk, salt, and peppers. Simmer for 20 minutes.
Yield: 14–16 servings

CREAM OF POTATO SOUP

8 slices bacon
1 cup water
3 medium potatoes, cubed
½ cup chopped onion
1 (10¾-ounce) can cream of chicken soup
1 (8-ounce) container sour cream
1½ cups milk
For garnish: parsley flakes

Fry bacon in a large boiler. Drain, crumble,
and set aside. Drain pan, but do not wash. Add
water, cubed potatoes, and onion, and bring to
a boil. Lower heat and simmer, covered, for 20
minutes. Stir in soup and sour cream. Gradually
add milk. Simmer until hot. Sprinkle parsley and
bacon on top.
Yield: 10–12 servings

CRABMEAT AND BRIE SOUP

1 small onion, minced

1 stalk celery, minced

1½ sticks butter

½ cup all-purpose flour

2 cups each: chicken broth, half-and-half, and heavy cream

½ cup plus 2 tablespoons Chardonnay wine

½ pound Brie cheese, cut into small pieces (rind removed)

1 pound crabmeat, picked over

Sauté onion and celery in butter for 5 minutes. Add flour, and cook for 5 additional minutes. Stir in chicken broth, half-and-half, and cream. Stir until smooth and thickened. Add wine and Brie. Stir until Brie is melted. Stir in crabmeat.

Yield: 8–10 servings

NAVY BEAN SOUP

1 small onion, chopped

¼ cup chopped bell pepper

⅓ cup chopped celery

1 tablespoon butter

1½ cups cooked and chopped ham

2 (16-ounce) cans navy beans, drained

2 cups half-and-half

½ cup water

Salt and black pepper to taste

Sauté onion, bell pepper, and celery in butter until tender. Add ham and lightly sauté. Add navy beans and half-and-half; then gradually add water. Add salt and pepper and stir well. Simmer for 1 hour over low heat.

Yield: 6 servings

Crabmeat and Brie Soup

Cool Strawberry Soup

COOL STRAWBERRY SOUP

1 (24-ounce) package frozen strawberries, thawed
2 cups fresh strawberries
½ cup sugar
2 cups heavy cream
1 quart milk
½ cup sour cream
For garnish: fresh strawberries and mint

In food processor, purée packaged and fresh berries. In a bowl, blend strawberry purée, sugar, cream, milk, and sour cream until smooth. Chill; stir before serving. Garnish with fresh strawberry halves and mint.
Yield: 16 servings

CUCUMBER SOUP

3 cucumbers, peeled and seeded
3 cups plain yogurt
1 tablespoon chopped dill
2 teaspoons chopped mint
2 teaspoons lime juice
Salt and black pepper to taste

In food processor, purée cucumbers. Add yogurt, herbs, and lime juice. Season with salt and pepper.
Yield: 6 servings

COOL MELON SOUP

This soup is so sweet and delicious!

4 cups chopped honeydew, cantaloupe, or
*   watermelon, seeds removed*
2 cups vanilla ice cream, softened
For garnish: fresh mint and small piece of melon

In food processor, purée melon pieces. Transfer to bowl, and stir in ice cream. Garnish with mint and small piece of melon.
Yield: 6–8 servings

PEACH SOUP

This is a great beginning for a ladies' luncheon.

3 cups peeled and chopped fresh peaches
1 tablespoon lemon juice
1 cup peach nectar
1 cup plain yogurt
½ teaspoon almond extract
For garnish: fresh mint and peach slices

In food processor, purée peaches and lemon juice. Transfer to bowl and stir in peach nectar, yogurt, and almond extract. Chill, and serve garnished with mint and peach slices.
Yield: 4–6 servings

SOUR CHERRY SOUP

1 pound fresh cherries, pitted
½ teaspoon cinnamon
¼ cup sugar
2 tablespoons water
2 cups red wine
2 cups half-and-half
For garnish: fresh mint and cherries with stems

In a saucepan, bring cherries, cinnamon, sugar, and water to a boil. Boil 5 minutes, add wine, and return to boil. Reduce heat, and simmer for 5 minutes. Cool and chill. Stir in half-and-half, and garnish with fresh mint and a cherry.
Yield: 6–8 servings

Smoked Chicken Salad

SALADS

Smoked Chicken Salad 55

Chicken Salad Veronique 55

Tropical Chicken Salad 55

French Chicken Salad 55

Shrimp Cocktail 56

Shrimp and Mango Salsa
Salad 56

Shrimp Mold 56

West Indies Salad 56

Caprese Salad 59

Combination Salad 59

Layered Club Salad 59

Fig Salad 60

Greens and Fruit with Citrus
Dressing 60

Balsamic Pear Vinaigrette with
Baby Greens, Blue Cheese,
and Candied Walnuts 61

Spring Mix with Sweet Paprika
Vinaigrette 61

Grilled Chicken Salad with
Lemon Vinaigrette 62

Oriental Chicken Salad with
Wonton Wrappers 63

Lebanese Salad 64

Bow Tie Pasta 64

Roasted Corn Salad 64

Creamy Chicken
Pasta Salad 64

Shrimp and Blueberry Coleslaw
with Maple Vinaigrette 65

Tamra's Coleslaw 65

Stuffed Eggs 67

Shrimp Deviled Eggs 67

Cream Cheese Stuffed Eggs 67

New Potato Salad 67

Cherry Salad 68

Lemon Ro-Tel Congealed
Salad 68

Green Fruit Salad 68

Spiced Fruit Dressing 68

Orange Yogurt Dressing 68

Honey Lime Fruit Dressing 69

Fresh Berries with
Lime-Sugar Glaze 69

Tropical Chicken Salad

SMOKED CHICKEN SALAD

4 chicken breasts, with skin and bones
1½ cups Allegro Original Marinade
¾ cup Hellmann's mayonnaise
Black pepper to taste
1 teaspoon prepared mustard
½ cup chopped sweet pickles
1 tablespoon dill pickle juice
2 ribs celery, finely chopped
1 teaspoon lemon juice
For garnish: real bacon bits

Marinate chicken breasts in Allegro Original Marinade for 1 hour. Smoke chicken on grill till internal temperature reaches 160–165 degrees. Remove from grill, cover with foil, and let rest 10 minutes. Chop chicken into bite-size pieces. Add remaining ingredients, and mix well. Chill and serve in lettuce cup. Sprinkle with bacon.
Yield: 8 servings

CHICKEN SALAD VERONIQUE

Ladies love this special chicken salad.

4 cups cooked and chopped chicken
1 cup halved seedless green grapes
1 cup slivered almonds, toasted
½ cup chopped celery
½ teaspoon celery salt
½ cup each: mayonnaise and lemon yogurt
1 tablespoon white wine
½ teaspoon prepared mustard
Leaf lettuce
For garnish: green grapes and strawberries

In a medium bowl, toss chicken, grapes, almonds, celery, and celery salt. In a small bowl, mix mayonnaise, yogurt, wine, and mustard. Fold mayonnaise mixture into chicken mixture. Chill until serving time.
Yields: 6–8 servings

TROPICAL CHICKEN SALAD

4 cups cooked and chopped chicken
¾ cup chopped celery
1 cup slivered almonds, lightly toasted
1 (8-ounce) can sliced water chestnuts, drained
1 (20-ounce) can pineapple chunks, drained
1 pound green or red grapes, divided
Black and white pepper to taste
1½ cups Hellmann's mayonnaise
1 tablespoon soy sauce
1 teaspoon curry
For garnish: lettuce, cantaloupe, frosted grapes, and sliced almonds

Combine chicken, celery, almonds, water chestnuts, pineapple, half of grapes, and peppers. For dressing, whisk together mayonnaise, soy sauce, and curry. Stir dressing mixture into chicken mixture. Serve salad on lettuce with cantaloupe slices. Garnish with frosted grapes and slivered almonds.
Yield: 12 servings

For frosted grapes, wet grapes, and dip in lime Jell-O mix. Dry on wire rack.

FRENCH CHICKEN SALAD

6 cups cooked and chopped chicken
1 stalk celery, diced
½ medium-size red bell pepper, diced
2 boiled eggs, chopped
1½ cups mayonnaise
1 teaspoon Dijon mustard
1 tablespoon yellow mustard
¾ cup sweet pickle relish
1 teaspoon sugar
Seasoned salt and black pepper to taste

Mix all ingredients and serve on a bed of lettuce.
Yield: about 12 servings

SHRIMP COCKTAIL

½ cup chili sauce
¼ teaspoon sugar
1 tablespoon horseradish
Juice of 1 lemon
½ teaspoon minced garlic
1 teaspoon Worcestershire sauce
½ teaspoon Tabasco sauce
1 teaspoon chopped cilantro
Salt and black pepper to taste
Shredded lettuce
24 steamed, deveined shrimp with tails

For sauce, combine chili sauce, sugar, horseradish, lemon juice, garlic, Worcestershire, Tabasco, cilantro, salt, and pepper. Pour 1 tablespoon of sauce on shredded lettuce in glass. Arrange shrimp around the rim.
Yield: 4 servings

🎗 SHRIMP AND MANGO SALSA SALAD

1 pound shrimp, peeled and deveined
1 tablespoon butter
1 clove garlic, minced
2 ripe mangos, peeled and cubed
1 cup chopped tomatoes
⅓ cup diced red onion
1 cup chopped cilantro
¼ teaspoon cumin
Juice of 1 lime
1 jalapeño, finely diced
Salt and black pepper to taste
Mixed spring greens

Sauté shrimp in butter and garlic until pink, about 5 minutes; set aside. Combine mangos, tomatoes, onion, and cilantro. Add cumin, lime juice, and jalapeño. Fold in shrimp and adjust taste with salt and pepper. Serve chilled over spring greens.
Yield: 4–6 servings

SHRIMP MOLD

2 (¼-ounce) envelopes plain gelatin
½ cup cold water
1 (10¾-ounce) can tomato soup
2 (3-ounce) packages cream cheese, softened
1 tablespoon lemon juice
1 cup mayonnaise
¼ cup chopped green pepper
½ cup chopped celery
1 pound shrimp, cooked, deveined, and chopped
Salt and white pepper to taste
Assorted crackers

Soften gelatin in water. Heat soup in the top of a double boiler. Add gelatin. Stir until dissolved. Remove from heat, and add cream cheese. With mixer, beat until cream cheese is melted; cool. Fold in lemon juice, mayonnaise, vegetables, and shrimp; add salt and pepper. Pour into 1 large mold or 12 individual molds and chill several hours to overnight. Serve with crackers.
Yield: 12 servings

WEST INDIES SALAD

1 pound jumbo lump crabmeat, shells removed
1 medium onion, chopped
1 bunch fresh parsley, minced
½ cup oil
¼ cup white vinegar
Juice of 1 lemon
1 tablespoon Tabasco sauce
2 teaspoons Worcestershire sauce
Salt and black pepper to taste

In a bowl, place crabmeat, onion, and parsley. Pour oil, vinegar, lemon juice, and sauces over crabmeat mixture. Cover with plastic wrap and chill. When ready to serve, stir and season with salt and pepper.
Yield: 4–6 servings

Shrimp Cocktail

Caprese Salad

CAPRESE SALAD

This little salad is an impressive presentation.

4 Roma tomatoes
8 ounces mozzarella cheese, cut into blocks
Spring mix salad greens
4 ounces mozzarella cheese, shredded
¼ cup chopped fresh basil
Seasoned salt and ground black pepper to taste
2 tablespoons olive oil

Hollow out tomatoes and fill with cheese blocks. Place on a bed of greens and shredded cheese. Season with basil, salt, and pepper, and drizzle with olive oil.
Yield: 4 servings

COMBINATION SALAD

1 head lettuce, broken into bite-size pieces
2 tomatoes, chopped
1 cucumber, diced
1 cup sliced celery
2 tablespoons chopped mint
2 tablespoons chopped parsley
1 teaspoon minced garlic
Juice of 2 lemons
3 tablespoons olive oil
Salt and black pepper to taste

Combine lettuce, tomatoes, cucumbers, celery, mint, and parsley. For dressing, mix together garlic, lemon juice, olive oil, salt, and pepper. Chill. Drizzle salad with dressing just before serving.
Yield: 6 servings

LAYERED CLUB SALAD

1 (8½-ounce) package cornbread mix, prepared according to package directions
1 (16-ounce) bottle peppercorn ranch salad dressing
¼ cup milk
¼ cup grated Parmesan cheese
4 cups shredded lettuce
2 cups chopped Boar's Head maple turkey
1 large bell pepper, chopped
2 heirloom tomatoes, chopped
1 Vidalia onion, sliced
2 cups grated Swiss cheese
1 (3-ounce) package real bacon bits
2 green onions, sliced

Crumble cornbread. Thin bottled dressing with milk, and add Parmesan cheese; set aside. Layer half of each, cornbread, lettuce, turkey, bell pepper, tomatoes, onion, Swiss cheese, and bacon bits. Repeat layers and drizzle with half of dressing. Cover and chill. Just before serving, sprinkle with green onions and remaining dressing mixture.
Yield: 24 servings

Fig Salad

FIG SALAD

This salad is as easy as slicing a fig.

6 ripe figs, sliced
½ cup unsalted peanuts, toasted
Spring mix greens
1 tablespoon raspberry vinegar
¼ cup peanut oil
Salt and black pepper to taste
For garnish: fresh mint

Place figs and peanuts on greens. Whisk vinegar, oil, and seasonings together, and drizzle over salad.
Yield: 6 servings

GREENS AND FRUIT WITH CITRUS DRESSING

1 bag each: spring greens and spinach
1 (15-ounce) can Mandarin oranges, drained
1 cup fresh blueberries
1 avocado, pitted and sliced
1 cup almond slivers, toasted

Arrange greens, spinach, fruits, and almonds on plates. Dress with Citrus Dressing.
Yield: 8 servings

CITRUS DRESSING:
¾ cup olive oil
¼ cup cider vinegar
Juice of 1 orange, 1 lime, and 1 lemon
1 tablespoon sugar
Salt and white pepper to taste

In jar with lid, combine ingredients, shake, and chill.

BALSAMIC PEAR VINAIGRETTE WITH BABY GREENS, BLUE CHEESE, AND CANDIED WALNUTS

1 bag mixed baby greens or spinach
4 pears, thinly sliced
6 ounces blue cheese, crumbled

Combine all ingredients. Top with 2 cups Candied Walnuts and Balsamic Pear Vinaigrette.
Yield: 6 servings

CANDIED WALNUTS:

9 tablespoons sugar, divided
3 tablespoons orange juice
2 cup walnut halves
½ teaspoon cinnamon

Preheat oven to 350 degrees. Line cookie sheet with greased foil. In a large skillet over medium heat, combine 6 tablespoons sugar and orange juice. Bring to a simmer; add walnuts; heat until sugar is absorbed and nuts begin to caramelize, about 2 minutes, stirring constantly. In a small bowl, combine remaining 3 tablespoons sugar and cinnamon. Toss walnuts in sugar mixture. Place on cookie sheet. Bake until toasted, about 5 minutes. Set aside to cool.

BALSAMIC PEAR VINAIGRETTE:

2 tablespoons wine vinegar
1 teaspoon Dijon mustard
Salt and black pepper to taste
6 tablespoons oil

Combine vinegar, mustard, and seasonings. Slowly whisk in oil. Allow dressing to rest a few hours at room temperature. Whisk again just before use.

SPRING MIX WITH SWEET PAPRIKA VINAIGRETTE

SALAD MIX:

½ stick butter
1 cup coarsely chopped pecans
1 package ramen noodles, crushed (seasoning packet discarded)
1 bag spring salad mix
1 Granny Smith apple, chopped
½ cup dried craisins

Melt butter in skillet; add nuts and ramen noodles, and cook on low heat until lightly toasted. Set aside to cool. Place salad greens on individual serving plates or in a large bowl. Top with apple, craisins, and nut mixture. Drizzle with Sweet Paprika Vinaigrette just before serving.
Yield: 6 servings

You may use fresh strawberries or Mandarin oranges in place of the apples and craisins.

SWEET PAPRIKA VINAIGRETTE:

2½ tablespoons cider vinegar
2½ teaspoons honey
½ teaspoon lemon juice
½ teaspoon paprika
⅓ cup sugar
½ teaspoon dry mustard
½ teaspoon celery seeds
½ teaspoon dried or minced onion
½ cup vegetable oil

Mix all ingredients, except the oil, in a pint jar. Heat in the microwave for 30–45 seconds. Add oil and shake well. Dressing can be made ahead and refrigerated. When ready to serve, warm in the microwave for 30–45 seconds and shake well. The more you shake, the thicker it will become.

GRILLED CHICKEN SALAD WITH LEMON VINAIGRETTE

4 boneless, skinless chicken breasts
¼ cup olive oil
1 cup lemon juice
½ tablespoon lemon pepper
½ cup Worcestershire sauce
1 each: red and yellow bell pepper, sliced
1 cup sugar snap peas, cleaned
1 cup crumbled goat cheese
¼ cup capers, drained and rinsed

Marinate chicken in mixture of olive oil, lemon juice, lemon pepper, and Worcestershire in a zipper bag 8 hours or overnight. Heat grill to medium. Cook chicken 8–10 minutes per side, until cooked through. Slice, and chill.

Toss sliced chicken, peppers, and sugar snap peas with Lemon Vinaigrette. Top with goat cheese and capers. Serve immediately.
Yield: 6–8 servings

LEMON VINAIGRETTE:
½ cup olive oil
½ cup fresh lemon juice
1 teaspoon kosher salt
1 teaspoon freshly ground pepper
1 each: clove garlic and shallot, finely chopped
1 tablespoon mayonnaise
Salt and black pepper to taste

Whisk together until combined.

ORIENTAL CHICKEN SALAD WITH WONTON WRAPPERS

Serve this salad with painted fortune cookies as placecard holders.

1 (12-ounce) package wonton wrappers
8 ounces fresh snow peas, with ends trimmed
8 cups mixed spring greens
2 cups fresh baby spinach
2 green onions, chopped
2 (11-ounce) cans Mandarin orange slices, drained
8 grilled chicken breasts, sliced into strips
½ cup sesame seeds, toasted
1 (9¼-ounce) can cashews

To deep-fry wonton wrappers, heat 1½ inches of oil to 375 degrees in wok or large skillet. Deep-fry wontons for 2–3 minutes until golden brown and crisp. Drain, and set aside. Cook fresh snow peas in boiling water for 1 minute. Drain; rinse under cold water, and pat dry. Combine peas, spring greens, spinach, onions, and orange slices.

Top with grilled chicken strips. Toss with Sweet and Sour Salad Dressing. Sprinkle with toasted sesame seeds, cashews, and fried wonton wrappers.
Yield: 8 servings

SWEET AND SOUR DRESSING:

½ cup wine vinegar
¾ cup sugar
3 teaspoons soy sauce
¼ teaspoon ground ginger
Salt and white pepper to taste
1 cup vegetable oil

Combine vinegar, sugar, soy sauce, and spices in a small mixing bowl. Add oil gradually, beating constantly with a wire whisk.
Yield: 2½ cups

 LEBANESE SALAD

1 pound red potatoes
½ cup chopped fresh parsley
2 tablespoons chopped mint
For garnish: 1 tomato, cut into wedges

Rinse and scrub potatoes. Cover potatoes with cold water to about one inch above the potatoes, and bring to a boil, uncovered, on high heat. Reduce heat to medium-low, and simmer potatoes until just tender, about 15 minutes. Drain and cool. Peel and dice potatoes into bowl. Add parsley and mint and toss with Dressing. Chill until ready to serve. Before serving, toss again. Serve with tomato wedges.
Yield: 4–6 servings

DRESSING:

2 cloves garlic, crushed
3 tablespoons olive oil
Juice of 3 lemons
Salt to taste

Combine garlic, oil, lemon juice, and salt.

BOW TIE PASTA

2 grilled chicken breasts, chopped
1 (16-ounce) package bow tie pasta, cooked al dente
1 (14-ounce) can artichoke hearts, drained
1 (4-ounce) jar chopped pimientos, drained
6 green onions, chopped
1 cup halved cherry tomatoes
½ cup olive oil
3 tablespoons mayonnaise
3 tablespoons lemon juice
2 tablespoons Greek seasoning

Combine chicken, pasta, artichoke hearts, pimientos, green onions, and tomatoes; set aside. For dressing, combine olive oil, mayonnaise, lemon juice, and seasoning. Toss chicken mixture with dressing.
Yield: 4 servings

 ROASTED CORN SALAD

2 cups fresh corn cut from the cob, or
*   1 (16-ounce) bag frozen whole-kernel*
1 tablespoon butter
1 avocado, pitted and diced into ½-inch pieces
½ cup finely diced red onion
½ cup diced roasted red peppers
⅓ cup mayonnaise
Zest and juice of 1 lime
¾ teaspoon ground cumin
1 tablespoon chopped fresh parsley
Salt to taste
For garnish: fresh parsley

Sauté corn in butter 5–8 minutes. Add avocado, onion, and peppers while corn is still warm; set aside. Mix together mayonnaise, lime zest and juice, cumin, parsley, and salt. Pour over corn mixture, and stir. Garnish with parsley.
Yield: 8–10 servings

CREAMY CHICKEN PASTA SALAD

2 chicken breasts, cooked and chopped
1 (12-ounce) bag multicolored rotini pasta, cooked and drained
1 (20-ounce) can chunk pineapple, drained and halved
2 cups halved seedless red grapes
1 Granny Smith apple, unpeeled and chopped
3 stalks celery, chopped
1 (8-ounce) can water chestnuts, drained and chopped
¾ cup ranch salad dressing
¾ cup mayonnaise
Salt and black pepper to taste

Combine chicken, pasta, pineapple, grapes, apple, celery, and water chestnuts. Whisk dressing with mayonnaise; pour over chicken and pasta mixture, and mix gently. Salt and pepper to taste. Chill until serving.
Yield: 8–10 servings

🎗 SHRIMP AND BLUEBERRY COLESLAW WITH MAPLE VINAIGRETTE

COLESLAW:

1 (12-ounce) bag coleslaw, or 8 cups shredded cabbage and carrots

1 pound cooked shrimp, deveined and tails removed (if over 2 inches, cut in half)

4 green onions, chopped, all of white and halfway up green tops

½ cup unsalted slivered almonds, toasted

¼ cup each: chopped fresh cilantro and chopped fresh basil

1 cup fresh blueberries, washed and drained (may use dried cranberries)

For salad, combine coleslaw, shrimp, onions, and almonds. One hour before serving, pour dressing on coleslaw; mix well. Add cilantro, basil, and blueberries; lightly toss.
Yield: 12–16 servings

MAPLE VINAIGRETTE:

4 tablespoons pure maple syrup

2 medium limes, zest to make 2 teaspoons, juiced to make 3 tablespoons

2 tablespoons extra light olive oil

1 teaspoon hot sauce

Whisk syrup, zest, juice, oil, and hot sauce.

🎗 TAMRA'S COLESLAW

3 packages shredded cabbage

¾ cup mayonnaise

1 (1-ounce) package dry ranch salad dressing mix

2 tomatoes, diced

2 cucumbers, peeled and diced

Salt and black pepper to taste

Rinse and drain cabbage. Add mayonnaise by the spoonful until desired moistness is achieved. Sprinkle salad dressing mix over cabbage mixture. Gently mix in tomatoes and cucumbers. Add salt and pepper to taste. Chill and stir before serving.
Yield: 12 servings

Shrimp and Blueberry Coleslaw with Maple Vinaigrette

STUFFED EGGS

These are the stuffed eggs my family loves best.

6 hard-cooked eggs, peeled and halved lengthwise
2 tablespoons butter, room temperature
2 tablespoons cubed dill pickles
6 tablespoons mayonnaise
1 teaspoon lemon juice
Salt and black and cayenne pepper to taste
For garnish: parsley and paprika

Remove yolks, and press through sieve; set aside whites. Stir in remaining ingredients. Pipe or spoon yolk mixture into whites. Garnish with parsley and paprika. Chill until serving.
Yield: 12 egg halves

SHRIMP DEVILED EGGS

6 hard-cooked eggs, peeled and halved lengthwise
¼ cup mayonnaise
2 teaspoons Dijon mustard
1½ teaspoons fresh lemon juice
1 teaspoon horseradish
¼ pound shrimp, cooked, peeled, deveined, and finely chopped
1 green onion, chopped
¾ teaspoon dried dill
Salt and black pepper to taste
For garnish: 12 whole cooked shrimp and fresh dill

Remove yolks, and press through sieve; set aside whites. Stir in remaining ingredients. Pipe or spoon yolk mixture into whites. Garnish with shrimp and dill. Chill until serving.
Yield: 12 egg halves

CREAM CHEESE STUFFED EGGS

6 hard-cooked eggs, peeled and halved lengthwise
1 (3-ounce) package cream cheese, softened
½ cup mayonnaise
1 teaspoon Dijon mustard
¼ teaspoon Worcestershire sauce
½ teaspoon Tabasco sauce
Salt and black pepper to taste
2 tablespoons sweet pickle relish

Remove yolks, and press through sieve; set aside whites. With electric mixer, combine cream cheese, mayonnaise, mustard, sauces, salt, and pepper. Stir in yolks and relish. Pipe or spoon yolk mixture into whites. Chill until serving.
Yield: 12 egg halves

NEW POTATO SALAD

6 strips bacon, fried, and cut into large chunks
1 (16-ounce) bottle bacon ranch salad dressing
1 cup mayonnaise
1 cup chopped green onion tops
4 hard-cooked eggs, grated
¼ cup red wine vinegar
Dill weed, celery seeds, salt, and black pepper to taste
5 pounds new potatoes, skins on, boiled, and cut into chunks

Combine all ingredients except potatoes, and mix well. Add potatoes and gently toss to coat.
Yield: 16–24 servings

CHERRY SALAD

This salad is a family favorite.

1 (21-ounce) can cherry pie filling
½ cup sugar
1 (3-ounce) package instant cherry Jell-O
1 (8-ounce) can crushed pineapple, drained
½ cup chopped pecans

Heat pie filling and sugar in a saucepan over medium heat or in microwave until it begins to boil. Stir in Jell-O until dissolved. Stir in pineapple and pecans. Pour into 8x8-inch Pyrex dish or 8 greased molds. Chill.
Yield: 8 servings

LEMON RO-TEL CONGEALED SALAD

This is an easy version of tomato aspic.

1 (10-ounce) can Ro-Tel tomatoes, drained
1 (8-ounce) package cream cheese, softened
½ cup milk
1 (3-ounce) package lemon Jell-O
½ cup chopped bell pepper
½ cup chopped celery
½ cup chopped onion
½ cup chopped pecans
½ cup mayonnaise

Combine tomatoes, cream cheese, and milk in a saucepan. Heat and stir until melted. Remove from heat and stir in Jell-O. Cool, and stir in bell pepper, celery, onion, pecans, and mayonnaise. Pour into 8x8-inch Pyrex dish or 8 greased molds. Chill overnight.
Yield: 8 servings

GREEN FRUIT SALAD

1 honeydew melon, cut into balls
2 green apples, unpeeled and chopped
2 kiwis, peeled and sliced
4 ounces seedless green grapes
For garnish: fresh mint and slivered orange rind

Combine prepared fruit with Syrup Dressing. Chill. Serve with fresh mint and orange rind.
Yield: 4–6 servings

SYRUP DRESSING:
Rind of 1 orange
⅔ cup white wine
⅔ cup water
4–5 tablespoons honey
Fresh mint sprigs

Pare orange rind using a potato peeler. Put the rind in a saucepan with wine, water, and honey. Bring to a boil, and simmer 10 minutes. Remove from heat; add mint. Strain cooled dressing, discarding orange rind and mint.

SPICED FRUIT DRESSING

½ cup white wine
½ cup honey
½ teaspoon cinnamon
¼ teaspoon allspice
3 tablespoons amaretto liqueur
For garnish: fresh mint

Combine ingredients, chill, and pour over seasonal, fresh fruit. Garnish with fresh mint.
Yield: 1½ cups

ORANGE YOGURT DRESSING

½ cup orange juice concentrate, thawed
3 tablespoons honey
1 (8-ounce) carton plain yogurt

Combine orange juice and honey. Fold in yogurt. Chill overnight. Serve on seasonal fruit.
Yield: 1½ cups

HONEY LIME FRUIT DRESSING

This is the perfect summer fruit dressing.

½ cup lime juice
½ cup oil
¼ cup sugar
¼ cup honey
1 teaspoon dry mustard
1 teaspoon paprika
1 teaspoon celery salt

Combine ingredients in a jar and shake. Chill, but bring to room temperature before serving with seasonal fruit.
Yield: 1½ cups

FRESH BERRIES WITH LIME-SUGAR GLAZE

Zest of 2 limes
Juice of 2 limes
1 cup each: fresh red raspberries, golden
   raspberries, blueberries, and blackberries
½ cup confectioners' sugar
1 cup heavy cream
1 teaspoon vanilla
For garnish: fresh mint and lime zest

Rim glasses by dipping in corn syrup, then colored sugar. Dry upside down on wax paper. Zest limes, and set aside for garnish. Juice limes. Toss berries with lime juice and confectioners' sugar until sugar has melted and berries are shiny. Chill. Whip cream with vanilla until soft peaks form. Serve berries with a dollop of whipped cream. Garnish with mint and lime zest.
Yield: 8 servings

Fresh Berries with Lime-Sugar Glaze

Turkey on Focaccia

SANDWICHES

Plantation Sandwiches

TURKEY ON FOCACCIA

This is a special turkey sandwich that becomes everyone's favorite.

1 loaf focaccia bread
Basil Mayonnaise
Leaf lettuce
3 Roma tomatoes, sliced
1 pound deli-style oven roasted turkey,
    thinly sliced
1 pound Havarti cheese, sliced

Slice bread and spread both sides with Basil Mayonnaise; layer with lettuce, tomatoes, and several slices of turkey and cheese.
Yield: 6 sandwiches

BASIL MAYONNAISE:

1 cup mayonnaise
2 tablespoons chopped fresh basil
1½ teaspoons lemon juice
Salt and black pepper to taste

Combine all ingredients.
Yield: 1¼ cups

PLANTATION SANDWICHES

1 (8½-ounce) package cornbread mix
2 (15-ounce) cans asparagus
12 slices smoked turkey
12–14 strips bacon, cooked and crumbled

Bake cornbread in 9-inch round iron skillet; cut into 6 wedges. Slice wedges in half. Warm asparagus in microwave. To assemble, place 1 piece of cornbread on plate; add 2 slices turkey and 3–4 pieces asparagus; top with cornbread. Spoon Easy Hollandaise Sauce on top, and sprinkle with crumbled bacon. Serve warm.
Yield: 6 sandwiches

EASY HOLLANDAISE SAUCE:

3 egg yolks
Juice of 2 lemons
1 stick butter, cut into 1-inch pieces

In a double boiler, place egg yolks and lemon juice in top bowl. Whisk eggs until mixture begins to thicken. Remove from heat, and continue to whisk, adding butter one piece at a time until completely incorporated. Serve immediately.
Yield: 1 cup

SPICY SOUTHERN FRIED GREEN TOMATO BLT

This is a very tasty sandwich with true southern flair.

6 slices thick-cut bacon
Rémoulade Sauce
2 medium green tomatoes, sliced
Vegetable oil, for frying
½ jalapeño, seeded and diced
½ cup yellow cornmeal
Salt and black pepper to taste
¾ cup buttermilk
4 slices sourdough bread, toasted
½ cup shredded lettuce
2 tablespoons sliced banana peppers, drained

Cook bacon in skillet until crispy; drain and cut each piece in half. Prepare Rémoulade Sauce and chill. For fried tomatoes, heat oil in fryer or deep cast-iron skillet until it reaches 350 degrees. Mix jalapeño and cornmeal together, and season with salt and pepper. Pour buttermilk into shallow dish. Dip tomato slices in buttermilk, then cornmeal mixture, and fry in oil. Cook for 1–1½ minutes, and drain. Spread top slice of toasted bread with Rémoulade Sauce. Place 6 half pieces of bacon on bottom bread slice, then top with 4 green tomatoes, shredded lettuce, and banana peppers. Add top slice of bread, and secure with toothpick.
Yield: 2 sandwiches

RÉMOULADE SAUCE:
¼ cup mayonnaise
1 tablespoon ketchup
1 teaspoon horseradish
¼ teaspoon capers, drained and rinsed
½ teaspoon Worcestershire sauce
¼ teaspoon chopped parsley
1 tablespoon lemon juice

Combine all ingredients.
Yield: 1 cup

Spicy Southern Fried Green Tomato BLT

CHICKEN SALAD WITH ALMONDS

3 cups chopped smoked chicken
¾ cup slivered almonds, toasted
1 cup mayonnaise
¾ cup dried cranberries
2 green onions, thinly sliced
1 cup diced celery
1 teaspoon dried dill
Salt, black pepper, and Tabasco sauce to taste

Combine all ingredients. Serve with leaf lettuce on croissant.
Yield: 6–8 servings

CHICKEN SALAD WITH CRANBERRIES AND PECANS

This is a very easy, sweet chicken salad.

1 (12½-ounce) can chicken breast, drained and chopped (1½ cups)
1 stalk celery, chopped
1 red apple, unpeeled and chopped
1 cup dried cranberries
1 cup chopped pecans, toasted
1 cup mayonnaise
2 teaspoons lemon juice
Black and white pepper to taste
1 teaspoon chopped parsley
For garnish: leaf lettuce

Combine ingredients. Serve with lettuce on wheat bread.
Yield: 6 sandwiches

Chicken Salad with Cranberries and Pecans

Pimiento Cheese

PIMIENTO CHEESE

1 (4-ounce) jar diced pimientos with juice
1 (16-ounce) package shredded mild Cheddar
  cheese
½ cup mayonnaise
½ teaspoon each: salt, white and black pepper

In a mixing bowl, stir ingredients together.
Serve with leaf lettuce on a croissant.
Yield: about 2½ cups

SPICY PIMIENTO CHEESE

1 (16-ounce) package shredded extra sharp
  Cheddar cheese
1 (4-ounce) jar diced pimientos with juice
5 heaping tablespoons mayonnaise
1 heaping teaspoon Zatarain's Creole Mustard
Salt, black pepper, and onion powder to taste

Blend all ingredients in food processor.
Yield: about 3 cups

CREAMY PIMIENTO SPREAD

This or any pimiento cheese sandwich is great
served with a slice or two of fried bacon.

3 cups grated mild Cheddar cheese
1 (4-ounce) jar whole pimientos with juice
½ cup Hellmann's mayonnaise, divided
1 teaspoon ground red pepper
1 teaspoon Worcestershire sauce

Pulse cheese and pimientos in the bowl of food
processor to finely chop the pimientos. Add ¼
cup mayonnaise, and pulse to combine. Add
pepper and Worcestershire. Pulse to mix until smooth. Pulse in remaining mayonnaise to
achieve consistency to spread easily.
Yield: about 3 cups

Egg and Olive Sandwiches

EGG AND OLIVE SANDWICHES

This is like the old drug store soda fountain favorite.

6 eggs, boiled, peeled, and chopped
¼ cup capers, drained and rinsed
½ cup chopped Spanish olives
1 rib celery, finely chopped
Salt, black pepper, and Tabasco sauce to taste
½ cup mayonnaise, mixed with 1 tablespoon fresh
  lemon juice
Leaf lettuce
12 white or wheat bread slices, lightly toasted

In bowl, mix together eggs, capers, olives, and celery. Blend in seasonings and mayonnaise, adding more, if needed. Place lettuce leaves on 6 slices of bread, and top with scoop of egg salad. Place remaining bread slices on each sandwich, and slice in half.
Yield: 6 sandwiches

RIVERA TUNA SANDWICHES

1 (6½-ounce) can tuna in oil
½ cup finely chopped pecans
¼ cup finely chopped pitted ripe olives
2 tablespoons chopped parsley
1 teaspoon capers, drained and rinsed
1 teaspoon grated onion
2 teaspoons Dijon mustard
2 tablespoons white wine vinegar
12 slices white bread
For garnish: sliced olives stuffed with pimientos

Mix together all ingredients except bread. Spread on 6 bread slices, then top with remaining bread slices, and cut in halves. Garnish with olive slices.
Yield: 6 sandwiches

BARBEQUE PORK TENDERLOIN SANDWICHES

2 (1-pound) pork tenderloins
2 cups tangy barbeque sauce, divided
Juice and zest of 1 orange
Juice and zest of 1 lemon
2 tablespoons Worcestershire sauce
3 cloves garlic, chopped
Salt and black pepper to taste
1 loaf French bread

Place tenderloins in a zipper bag. Mix 1 cup barbeque sauce, juice and zest of orange and lemon, Worcestershire, and garlic, and pour over tenderloins. Chill and marinate for several hours. Heat grill or grill pan to high heat. Remove tenderloins from the marinade and season with salt and pepper. Place on the rack or pan and cover; heat 10 minutes. Turn meat, reduce heat to medium-low, and cook an additional 10–15 minutes, or until meat thermometer registers 145 degrees for medium. Remove from heat, and tent with foil. Let meat rest for 10 minutes; slice.

Toast sliced French bread lightly under broiler. Top with sliced tenderloin, slaw, and remaining 1 cup barbeque sauce.
Yield: 6–8 servings

TANGY SLAW:

1 head cabbage, core removed and thinly sliced
½ head red cabbage, core removed and thinly sliced
½ red onion, thinly sliced
1 red bell pepper, thinly sliced
1 yellow bell pepper, thinly sliced
1 teaspoon celery seeds
1 teaspoon celery salt
¼ cup sugar
½ cup vinegar
½ cup mayonnaise
Salt and black pepper to taste

Toss all ingredients together and chill.
Yield: 6–8 servings

LOBSTER TACOS WITH MANGO SALSA AND JALAPEÑO HOLLANDAISE SAUCE

LOBSTER TACOS:
8 (6-inch) soft tortillas
1 (1- to 2-pound) cooked lobster, meat removed and chopped
For garnish: chopped chives

Prepare Mango Salsa and Jalapeño Hollandaise Sauce, and set aside. Turn the oven setting to broil. Place the soft tortillas on a cookie sheet and put 1½ tablespoons chopped lobster in the center of each taco. Top with 1 tablespoon Mango Salsa and 1 tablespoon of the Jalapeño Hollandaise Sauce. Place tacos under broiler for 2 minutes. Fold each taco in half, and sprinkle with chopped chives. Serve immediately with additional salsa.
Yield: 8 tacos

MANGO SALSA:
1 mango, chopped
1 small red onion, chopped
1 red bell pepper, chopped
1 yellow bell pepper, chopped
1 cucumber, peeled and chopped
2 jalapeño peppers, seeded and chopped
1 orange, peeled, seeded, and chopped
¼ cup chopped cilantro
½ cup chopped parsley
Juice of 2 limes
Salt and black pepper to taste

Combine all ingredients in a glass bowl. Chill until ready to serve.
Yield: 2 cups

JALAPEÑO HOLLANDAISE SAUCE:
3 egg yolks
½ jalapeño pepper, seeded and chopped
Juice of 1 lemon
1 stick cold butter, cut into pieces

In the top of a double boiler over barely simmering water, combine egg yolks, pepper, and lemon juice, whisking constantly. When mixture begins to thicken, cut heat to low and whisk in butter, one piece at a time, until incorporated and sauce is smooth. Remove from heat; set aside.
Yield: ¾ cup

CHICKEN WALDORF WRAPS

These are quick, easy, and delicious!

1 cup baby spinach
1 apple, cored and diced
2 cups chopped cooked chicken
½ cup toasted almonds
½ cup dried cherries
6 large flour tortillas

Combine the spinach, apple, and chicken; toss well. Toss with Yogurt Dressing. Stir in nuts and cherries. Place 3 tablespoonfuls of salad into the middle of each tortilla, and roll tightly.
Yield: 6 wraps

YOGURT DRESSING:
1 cup plain yogurt
Juice of 1 large orange
Salt and black and white pepper to taste

Combine yogurt, orange juice, salt and pepper.

Lobster Tacos with Mango Salsa and Jalapeño Hollandaise Sauce

SLIDERS

1 pound ground beef
Salt and black pepper to taste
Yellow onion, yellow and red bell peppers, sliced
12 small hamburger buns or rolls, toasted
Mayonnaise, mustard, and dill pickle slices

Preheat flat-top griddle. Form sliders by making thin patties. Salt and pepper both sides. Place on griddle with onion and bell peppers on top. Cook until first side is brown and cooked halfway through. Flip slider and cook with vegetables under the sliders until done. Place on toasted bun. Serve with condiments.
Yield: 12 sliders

MONTEREY JACK TURKEY BURGERS

1¼ pounds ground turkey
3 scallions, minced
1½ tablespoons Worcestershire sauce
1½ tablespoons ketchup
2 teaspoons steak seasoning
¼ teaspoon garlic powder
¼ teaspoon black pepper
½ cup shredded Monterey Jack cheese
12 small hamburger buns or rolls
Tomato slices, lettuce, pickles, onions, extra
*   Monterey Jack cheese slices*

Combine turkey, scallions, Worcestershire sauce, ketchup, and seasonings. Blend in cheese and form into 12 small patties. On ridged, greased grill pan over medium-high heat, cook patties, covered. Add ¼ cup of water to pan after burgers have been cooking about 3 minutes. Cook burgers 6–8 minutes per side, or until cooked through. Add another ¼ cup water to pan after you have flipped the burgers and they have been cooking 3 minutes on that side. (This really helps the burgers remain moist and juicy.) Serve with condiments of choice.
Yield: 12 small appetizer burgers

HAVARTI-BEEF SANDWICHES

These sandwiches are the perfect party fare.

2 (11-ounce) packages Parker House yeast rolls
1 (10-ounce) jar Durkee's Famous Sauce
1 (8-ounce) package sliced Havarti cheese
1½ pounds deli-style Boar's Head roast beef, thinly
*   sliced*
½ cup toasted and finely chopped walnuts
½ (18-ounce) jar apricot chutney or jam

Preheat oven to 300 degrees. Slice rolls in half, and spread bottom side with Durkee's spread, a cheese slice, several slices beef, and walnuts. Spread top side of roll with apricot chutney or jam, and place on sandwich. Place sandwiches back in pan, cover with foil, and heat for 20–25 minutes.
Yield: 32 sandwiches

ITALIAN BEEF SANDWICHES

1 (4-pound) rump roast
1 cup Worcestershire sauce
1 tablespoon parsley flakes
2 teaspoons basil
1 tablespoon Italian seasoning
2 teaspoons oregano
2 teaspoons Tabasco sauce
2 (24-ounce) packages tea biscuits
½ cup water

Preheat oven to 450 degrees. Place roast in baking pan, and pour Worcestershire over roast. Sprinkle with parsley, basil, Italian seasoning, and oregano. Drizzle with Tabasco. Cover and bake 15 minutes. Reduce heat to 250 degrees, and bake for 8 hours. Remove from oven and cut into pieces. Add water, cover, and return to oven for 4 more hours. Serve warm on biscuits.
Yield: 48 sandwiches

Sliders

HAM AND SWISS ROLLS

These are all-time favorites for parties and tailgating.

1 (16-ounce) canned ham
4 tablespoons Grey Poupon mustard, divided
2 tablespoons brown sugar
2 (11-ounce) packages Parker House yeast rolls
1 stick butter, softened
2 teaspoons poppy seeds
1 (16-ounce) package sliced Swiss cheese

Preheat oven to 275 degrees. Spread canned ham with 1 tablespoon mustard and brown sugar. Wrap in foil, and bake for 1 hour. Allow ham to cool. Chop ham into small pieces, and set aside. Preheat oven to 350 degrees. Without separating packages of rolls, slice horizontally with a sharp knife. Spread bottom and top sides of rolls with a mixture of butter, 3 tablespoons mustard, and poppy seeds. Place chopped ham on rolls; top with Swiss cheese slices. Replace tops of rolls; and separate rolls with a sharp knife. Bake in roll pan covered with foil for 12 minutes. Remove foil and bake 5 minutes longer.
Yield: 32 sandwiches

CONFETTI SANDWICHES

1 (8-ounce) package cream cheese, softened
½ cup mayonnaise
2 tablespoons olive juice
1 cup finely chopped pecans, divided
1 cup finely chopped olives with pimientos
Black and white pepper to taste
1 loaf white sandwich bread with crusts removed

Combine cream cheese, mayonnaise, and olive juice. Mix in pecans, olives, and peppers. Spread on bread and cut into tea sandwiches.
Yield: 48 tea sandwiches

DATE-NUT CHICKEN SANDWICHES

This sweet delight is great for showers and teas.

12 slices thin white bread, crusts removed
½ stick butter, softened
1 cup cooked and diced chicken
½ cup finely chopped dates
¼ cup finely chopped pecans
½ cup real bacon bits
½ cup mayonnaise
Salt and white pepper to taste

Butter each slice of bread. Combine chicken, dates, pecans, bacon bits, mayonnaise, salt, and pepper. Spread chicken mixture on 6 slices of bread. Top with remaining slices, and cut each into 4 small triangles.
Yield: 24 tea sandwiches

PINEAPPLE-NUT SANDWICHES

These sandwiches are pretty on raisin bread.

¼ cup evaporated milk
2 (8-ounce) packages cream cheese, softened
1 cup crushed pineapple, drained
½ cup chopped pecans
1 loaf raisin bread

Cream together milk and cream cheese. Add pineapple and nuts. Blend well. Spread on raisin bread, and cut into tea sandwiches.
Yield: 48 tea sandwiches

TOMATO ROUNDS

Everyone loves these tomato sandwich rounds. They are the perfect pick-up for buffets.

2 loaves white bread
1 (8-ounce) package cream cheese, softened
1 teaspoon lemon juice
2 (1-ounce) packages original dry ranch dressing mix
6 small fresh tomatoes, thinly sliced and drained
For garnish: fresh chopped basil or parsley

Cut rounds from bread with cookie cutter a little larger than tomato slices. Combine cream cheese, lemon juice, and ranch dressing mix. Spread bread rounds with cream cheese mixture. Refrigerate rounds on trays with damp paper towels in bottom and wax paper between the layers. Add tomato slices just before serving. Garnish with basil or parsley.
Yield: 40 tea sandwiches

SHRIMP SANDWICHES

1 (6-ounce) can tiny shrimp, drained and chopped
1 tablespoon lemon juice
1 (8-ounce) package cream cheese, softened
1½ cups mayonnaise, divided
1 tablespoon Worcestershire sauce
1 loaf white bread, crusts removed
½ cup finely chopped fresh parsley

Sprinkle shrimp with lemon juice; set aside. Combine cream cheese, 1 cup mayonnaise, and Worcestershire. Stir in shrimp. Spread on bread and cut into small tea sandwiches. Roll edges first in mayonnaise, then in parsley.
Yield: 36 tea sandwiches

CUCUMBER SANDWICHES

This is a delicious, easy version of the standard cucumber sandwiches always served at tea time.

1 loaf white bread
1 (8-ounce) package cream cheese, softened
1 teaspoon lemon juice
1 tablespoon dill
1 teaspoon lemon pepper
3 cucumbers, sliced and drained
For garnish: fresh dill

Cut rounds from bread with cookie cutter a little larger than cucumber slices. Combine cream cheese, lemon juice, dill, and lemon pepper. Spread bread rounds with cream cheese mixture. Refrigerate rounds on trays with damp paper towels in bottom and wax paper between the layers. Add cucumber slices just before serving. Garnish with dill.
Yield: 40 tea sandwiches

DILL PICKLE SANDWICHES

Great to serve for baby showers with sweets and ice cream.

1 (8-ounce) package cream cheese, softened
2 tablespoons mayonnaise
1 teaspoon grated onion
1 loaf white bread, crusts removed
1 (22-ounce) jar baby dill pickles

In a medium bowl, mix cream cheese, mayonnaise, and grated onion. Spread the mixture thinly on the white bread slices. Roll 1 baby dill pickle in each slice of bread. Place seam side down in plastic container with sealed cover. Chill overnight. To serve, slice each bread roll into 1-inch slices.
Yield: 40 tea sandwiches

Tomato Rounds

Kumquat Nut Scones with Orange Butter

BREAKFAST AND BRUNCH

Kumquat Nut Scones with
   Orange Butter 88

Blueberry Bars 88

Puff Pastry with Cream and
   Raspberries 88

Quiche Lorraine 91

Cheese Grits 91

Ham and Cheese Strata 91

Sausage and Cheese Squares 92

Spicy Bacon 92

Blueberry French Toast 92

Easy Cinnamon Rolls 92

Brunch Shrimp and Grits 93

Smoky Eggs Benedict over
   Cornbread Cakes 94

Tommy Toe Pie 95

Mexican Casserole 95

Baked Fruit 96

Apricot Bake 96

Grape Salad 96

Special Strawberries 96

Cranberry-Almond Granola 96

❀ KUMQUAT NUT SCONES WITH ORANGE BUTTER

These scones melt in your mouth with a burst of citrus!

7–8 fresh kumquats
1½ sticks butter, cut into pieces
⅓ cup sugar
2 cups all-purpose flour
4 teaspoons baking powder
½ cup coarsely chopped pecans
Orange juice to bind (about 2 tablespoons)
Additional melted butter and sugar

Wash kumquats, cut in half, and seed. Place in food processor and pulse several times until chopped. Set aside. In a mixer or food processor, cream butter and sugar. Add flour and baking powder until blended. Stir in kumquats and pecans. Add orange juice, a little at a time, to bind mixture. Mixture will be stiff. Knead a few times, wrap tightly in plastic wrap, and refrigerate overnight.

Preheat oven to 450 degrees. Roll out mixture into 1 large circle or 2 small circles about 1 inch thick on parchment-lined baking sheet. Slice into wedges. Pull each wedge away until there is a small space between wedges. Spread each wedge with melted butter, and sprinkle each with sugar.

Bake for 15 minutes until golden brown. Remove from oven and spread with Orange Butter.
Yield: 12 large scones or 24 small scones

ORANGE BUTTER:
1 stick butter, softened
1 tablespoon grated orange rind

Combine butter and rind. Chill until ready to serve. Bring to room temperature about 30 minutes before serving.
Yield: ½ cup

BLUEBERRY BARS

1 (8-ounce) can crescent rolls
½ cup plus 2 teaspoons sugar, divided
1 (8-ounce) package cream cheese, softened
½ teaspoon almond extract
1 pint fresh blueberries

Preheat oven to 350 degrees. Place half can of rolls in 6x10-inch dish greased with butter. Press together seams to make a solid sheet. With mixer, cream ½ cup sugar, cream cheese, and almond extract. Spread over dough. Lightly press blueberries over cream cheese mixture. Place remaining dough over blueberries, pinching seams together to make a smooth top crust. Sprinkle with remaining 2 teaspoons sugar. Bake 18–20 minutes or until golden brown.
Yield: 16–20 bars

PUFF PASTRY WITH CREAM AND RASPBERRIES

1 (8-ounce) package cream cheese, softened
½ cup sugar, divided
1 egg, separated
1 sheet puff pastry, thawed
1 cup raspberries

Preheat oven to 400 degrees. With mixer, beat cream cheese and ¼ cup sugar until light and fluffy. Add egg yolk. Lay sheet of puff pastry on a flat surface and cut into 12 small squares. Spoon one tablespoon of the cream cheese mixture down center of each square from corner to opposite corner. Press 4 berries into mixture. Fold opposite corners to center; wet point with water, and seal. Place on the greased baking sheet, brush with the egg white, and sprinkle with remaining ¼ cup sugar. Bake 15–17 minutes until golden brown.
Yield: 12 mini pastries

Blueberry Bars and Puff Pastry with Cream and Raspberries

Quiche Lorraine and Cheese Grits

QUICHE LORRAINE

1 (9-inch) rolled pie crust
1½ tablespoons butter
¼ cup chopped onion
1 (3-ounce) package real bacon bits
½ cup chopped cooked ham
¾ cup shredded Swiss cheese
3 eggs
¾ cup half-and-half
Salt, black and white pepper, and nutmeg to taste

Preheat oven to 350 degrees. Spread crust in greased 9-inch tart pan. Sauté onion in butter. Spread onion, bacon, ham, and cheese in crust. With mixer, beat eggs; stir in half-and-half and seasonings. Pour into shell. Bake 25–30 minutes until set.
Yield: 8 servings

CRAB QUICHE:
Replace ham with 1 (7-ounce) can crab, washed and drained.

ASPARAGUS AND ARTICHOKE QUICHE:
Replace ham with ½ cup cooked asparagus pieces and 1 (6-ounce) jar of chopped marinated artichoke hearts, drained.

CHEESE GRITS

1½ cups instant grits
3 cups chicken broth
1 (16-ounce) package shredded Velveeta cheese
1 (10-ounce) can Ro-Tel tomatoes, drained
1 (8-ounce) package cream cheese, softened
1 cup sour cream

Preheat oven to 350 degrees. Cook grits according to directions, substituting broth for water; set aside. Microwave cheese and tomatoes until melted. Stir in cream cheese and sour cream until combined. Stir in grits. Pour into greased 9x13-inch dish, or 12 greased molds. Bake for 20–30 minutes.
Yield: 12–16 servings

HAM AND CHEESE STRATA

For a wedding brunch, cut bread into hearts on the top.

1 (24-ounce) canned ham
1 tablespoon Grey Poupon mustard
2 tablespoons light brown sugar
12 slices white bread
1 (10-ounce) package frozen chopped broccoli, steamed
2 cups finely grated Cheddar cheese
6 eggs, beaten
3 cups half-and-half
Salt, black pepper, and white pepper to taste
2 tablespoons butter, melted

Preheat oven to 275 degrees. Spread mustard on canned ham, and sprinkle with brown sugar. Bake in foil for one hour. Cool, and cut into bite-sized pieces. Change oven temperature to 325 degrees. With a small heart-shaped cookie cutter, cut 2 small hearts from each slice of bread; set aside. Break remaining bread into small pieces, and place in a greased 9x13-inch baking dish. Layer ham, broccoli, and cheese. With electric mixer, beat eggs, half-and-half, salt, and peppers. Pour into casserole. Dip heart-shaped bread pieces into melted butter, and place on top of casserole. Bake for 45 minutes. Allow to cool 30 minutes, and cut into squares.
Yield: 12–16 servings

SAUSAGE AND CHEESE SQUARES

1 pound ground pork sausage
½ cup finely chopped onion
¼ cup grated Parmesan cheese
½ cup grated Cheddar cheese
1 egg, beaten
½ teaspoon Tabasco sauce
Salt and black pepper to taste
1 cup biscuit mix
¾ cup milk
¼ cup mayonnaise
1 egg yolk
1 tablespoon water

Preheat oven to 400 degrees. In skillet, brown sausage and onion; drain well. Add cheeses, egg, Tabasco, salt and pepper, and set aside. In a bowl, mix together biscuit mix, milk, and mayonnaise. Combine sausage mixture and biscuit mixture. Pour into a greased 9x9-inch baking dish. Combine egg yolk and water, and brush on top of sausage and cheese. Bake for 25–30 minutes. Cut into squares.
Yield: 6 servings

SPICY BACON

3 eggs
2 tablespoons dry mustard
⅛ teaspoon ground red pepper
2 tablespoons tarragon vinegar
1½ cups crushed buttery crackers
2 pounds thick bacon

Preheat oven to 350 degrees. In a large bowl, beat eggs and add dry mustard, red pepper, and vinegar. Place cracker crumbs on a large flat plate. One at a time, dip bacon strips in egg mixture, then dredge both sides in crumbs. Place bacon strips onto baking sheet with sides, lined with foil, and bake 30–40 minutes. Bacon will remain flat when cooked.
Yield: 16 servings

BLUEBERRY FRENCH TOAST

1 loaf French bread, cut into 1-inch cubes
8 eggs
1½ cups milk
½ teaspoon vanilla
¼ teaspoon salt
1 cup packed light brown sugar, divided
½ stick unsalted butter
1 cup each: pecans and blueberries
Maple syrup
For garnish: fresh blueberries and confectioners' sugar

Place bread into 12 buttered muffin tins. Whisk eggs, milk, vanilla, salt, and ¾ cup brown sugar. Pour over the bread; cover, and chill overnight. In the morning, preheat oven to 350 degrees. Heat butter and remaining ¼ cup brown sugar until melted. Remove from heat; add pecans and blueberries. Pour over bread. Bake 15–18 minutes. Serve with maple syrup; garnish with blueberries, and dust with confectioners' sugar.
Yield: 12 servings

EASY CINNAMON ROLLS

2 (8-ounce) cans crescent rolls
6 tablespoons butter, softened
⅓ cup packed brown sugar
1 teaspoon each: sugar and cinnamon

Form 4 rectangles from rolls. Combine butter, sugars, and cinnamon. Spread over rectangles and roll up. Cover with plastic wrap; chill. Preheat oven to 375 degrees. Remove rolls; cut each into 6 slices. Place in greased 9x13-inch baking dish; bake 15–18 minutes. Drizzle with Icing.
Yield: 24 rolls

ICING:
⅔ cup confectioners' sugar
1 tablespoon half-and-half
1 teaspoon vanilla
⅛ teaspoon salt

Whisk ingredients together until smooth.

BRUNCH SHRIMP AND GRITS

1½ pounds small shrimp, peeled and deveined

1½ tablespoons lemon juice

½ teaspoon Tabasco sauce

8 slices bacon, coarsely chopped (about 1 cup)

1/3 cup chopped green onions (white and tender green parts)

½ teaspoon minced garlic

2 tablespoons all-purpose flour

1 cup chicken broth

¼ cup half-and-half

Salt and black pepper to taste

In a bowl, toss shrimp with the lemon juice and Tabasco; set aside. For gravy, fry the bacon in a large skillet over medium heat until lightly browned, but not crispy. Stir in the green onions and garlic, and cook, stirring often, until softened, about 3 minutes. Sprinkle flour over onion mixture, stirring and scraping from the bottom of the pan until lightly browned, about 3 minutes. Stir in broth, half-and-half, salt, and pepper and cook, stirring, until the gravy thickens, about 5 minutes. Stir in the shrimp with accumulated liquid and cook until opaque, 3–5 minutes. Serve over hot Cheese Grits.
Yield: 6–8 servings

CHEESE GRITS:

1 cup quick grits

4 tablespoons butter

¾ cup shredded sharp white Cheddar cheese

½ cup grated Parmesan cheese

1 teaspoon ground red pepper

1 teaspoon paprika

Salt and black pepper to taste

Cook grits according to package directions. Stir in butter, cheeses, red pepper, and paprika. Season with salt and pepper to taste.

Smoky Eggs Benedict over Cornbread Cakes

 # SMOKY EGGS BENEDICT OVER CORNBREAD CAKES

CORNBREAD CAKES:

3 slices bacon
¼ red onion, diced
1 red bell pepper, diced
2 green onions, thinly sliced
1 jalapeño, seeded and diced
2 cloves garlic, minced
Salt and black pepper to taste
1 (8½-ounce) package cornbread mix, baked
3 eggs
1 cup black-eyed peas, cooked and drained
1½ teaspoons ground cumin
1 teaspoon paprika
¼ teaspoon Creole seasoning

Cook bacon until crispy; drain, crumble, and set aside. In remaining grease, sauté onion, jalapeño, and garlic for 5 minutes. Season with salt and pepper; cool. Purée crumbled cornbread and add eggs. Combine cornbread mixture, veggies, bacon, black-eyed peas, and remaining spices. Shape into 3-inch cakes, ¾ inches tall, and place on greased baking sheet. Chill 30 minutes. Preheat oven to 300 degrees. Fry cakes in butter until browned on both sides.

Return cakes to baking sheet and bake 10 minutes. Top each cake with a poached egg and Chipotle Hollandaise.
Yield: 6–8 servings

EASY CHIPOTLE HOLLANDAISE:

3 egg yolks
2 tablespoons lemon juice
¼ teaspoon salt
⅛ teaspoon ground red pepper
1 stick unsalted butter
¼ teaspoon finely ground dried chipotles, red pepper, or smoked paprika

Place yolks, lemon juice, salt, and red pepper in blender. Heat butter and chipotles in microwave until bubbly; set aside. With blender on high, pour butter mixture in a small stream while blender is running.

For poached eggs, in a saucepan bring water, 1 teaspoon white vinegar, and 1 teaspoon salt to a boil. Lower heat to a simmer. Crack egg into measuring cup; drop into water. Cook 3–4 minutes. Remove with slotted spoon.

TOMMY TOE PIE

5 tomatoes
1 (9-inch) deep-dish pie shell
½ cup shredded sharp Cheddar cheese
½ cup shredded white Cheddar cheese
¼ cup mayonnaise
1 tablespoon Dijon mustard
Salt and black pepper to taste
1 bunch green onions, chopped
½ cup shredded Parmesan cheese

The day before, slice tomatoes and drain on paper towels. Chill. Bake deep-dish pie shell according to package directions. Cool. Mix sharp Cheddar cheese, white Cheddar cheese, and mayonnaise. Set mixture aside. Spread the bottom of the pie shell with Dijon mustard. Place a layer of tomatoes, and then sprinkle with salt and pepper. Spread with half of the cheese and mayonnaise mixture. Sprinkle with chopped green onions. Repeat layers. End with ½ cup shredded Parmesan cheese on top. Bake at 375 degrees for 35–40 minutes.
Yield: 6 servings

MEXICAN CASSEROLE

This is an easy casserole that everyone enjoys.

1 pound ground turkey or ground round
1 (1¼-ounce) package taco seasoning mix
1 teaspoon water
6 eggs
1 (3-ounce) package cream cheese, softened
¼ cup heavy cream
1 (10-ounce) can Ro-Tel tomatoes
1 clove garlic, chopped
2 cups shredded Cheddar cheese, divided

Preheat oven to 350 degrees. Brown meat; stir in taco mix and water; set aside. Beat eggs; stir in cream cheese and cream. Add tomatoes, garlic, and 1½ cups cheese; mix well. Fold in meat mixture. Pour in greased 9x13-inch baking dish; top with remaining cheese. Bake 45 minutes or until brown. Cut into squares.
Yield: 12–16 servings

Tommy Toe Pie

BAKED FRUIT

3 pears, peeled and sliced
3 apples, peeled and sliced
1 cup cranberries
1 (21-ounce) can lemon pie filling
1 teaspoon ground cinnamon
½ teaspoon ground nutmeg

Preheat oven to 350 degrees. In an 8x8-inch baking dish, layer pears, apples, and cranberries; set aside. In a bowl, mix pie filling, cinnamon, and nutmeg, and pour over fruits. Cover and bake 1 hour or until fruits are just tender.
Yield: 8 servings

APRICOT BAKE

2 (15-ounce) cans apricot halves, drained
¾ cup light brown sugar, divided
1 cup buttery round cracker crumbs
1 stick margarine, melted

Preheat oven to 325 degrees. In a buttered 2-quart casserole, place apricots and sprinkle with sugar. Combine cracker crumbs with margarine, and crumble over fruit. Bake for 30–35 minutes. Serve hot or room temperature.
Yield: 8 servings

GRAPE SALAD

1 (8-ounce) package cream cheese, softened
2 cups sour cream
1 teaspoon vanilla
3 pounds green and red grapes, halved
1 cup brown sugar
1 cup chopped pecans

With mixer, beat cream cheese, sour cream, and vanilla until creamy. Fold in grapes. Pour into a 9x13-inch dish. Combine brown sugar and pecans, and spread over grapes and cream cheese mixture.
Yield: 12–16 servings

SPECIAL STRAWBERRIES

These are great with homemade pound cake.

3 pints fresh strawberries
½ cup raspberry jam
4 tablespoons sugar
¼ cup water
2 tablespoons orange juice

Wash and hull strawberries. Combine jam, sugar, and water in a saucepan, and simmer for 2 minutes. Add orange juice, and chill. Arrange berries in a bowl, and cover with sauce.
Yield: 3 pints strawberries

CRANBERRY-ALMOND GRANOLA

4 cups old-fashioned oats
1½ cups sliced almonds
½ cup packed light brown sugar
½ teaspoon salt
½ teaspoon ground cinnamon
¼ cup oil
¼ cup honey
1 teaspoon vanilla
1½ cups dried cranberries

Preheat oven to 300 degrees. In a bowl, combine oats, almonds, brown sugar, salt, and cinnamon. In a saucepan, warm oil and honey; stir in vanilla. Pour liquid mixture over the oat mixture, and stir gently with a wooden spoon; finish mixing by hand. Spread granola in a 1x10x15-inch baking pan lined with greased foil. Bake 30 minutes, stirring carefully every 10 minutes. Transfer pan to wire rack. Cool completely. Stir in dried cranberries. Seal granola in an airtight container. Store at room temperature for up to 1 week, or in freezer for up to 3 months.
Yield: 7½ cups

Special Strawberries

Beef Tenderloin with Caramelized
Onions and Herb Butter

MEATS

BEEF TENDERLOIN WITH CARAMELIZED ONIONS AND HERB BUTTER

4 (6- to 8-ounce) beef filets
Salt and cracked black pepper to taste
2 tablespoons lemon juice

Season filets with salt, pepper, and lemon juice. Heat grill or black iron skillet to medium-high heat. Cook for 4–5 minutes, until steak reaches desired temperature (140 degrees, rare; 170 degrees, well done). Keep warm. To serve, top with Caramelized Onions and Herb Butter.
Yield: 4 servings

CARAMELIZED ONIONS:
1 onion, chopped
2 tablespoons butter

Sauté onions in butter until golden brown.

HERB BUTTER:
6 tablespoons butter, softened
¼ cup chopped fresh parsley, thyme, basil, and
*   rosemary*
2 tablespoons Worcestershire sauce

Combine ingredients, and chill.

FIREMAN JOHN'S BEEF TENDERLOIN

1 (4- to 5-pound) beef tenderloin, trimmed
1 cup Worcestershire sauce
½ cup soy sauce
1 tablespoon each: black pepper, Lawry's Seasoned
*   Salt, lemon pepper, and garlic salt*
½ cup packed light brown sugar

Marinate tenderloin for 2–3 hours in a marinade made by mixing remaining ingredients. Cook on grill over direct heat for 20 minutes, turning every 5 minutes. Cut into steaks, and return to grill; cook to desired doneness.
Yield: 6–8 servings

PEPPER CHUTNEY BEEF TENDERLOIN

This tenderloin is so tender with a great blend of flavors.

1 (3- to 4-pound) beef tenderloin, trimmed
¾ cup unsweetened pineapple juice
½ cup Dale's Steak Seasoning
⅓ cup Worcestershire sauce
⅓ cup port wine
¼ cup lemon juice
2 teaspoons seasoned salt
1 teaspoon each: black pepper, lemon pepper, and
*   dry mustard*
2 teaspoons ground black pepper
6 slices bacon
1 (9-ounce) jar pepper chutney

Place tenderloin in zipper bag. Combine juice, steak seasoning, Worcestershire, wine, lemon juice, seasoned salt, black pepper, lemon pepper, and dry mustard. Pour over meat, and marinade in refrigerator for 8 hours, turning occasionally. Drain; reserve marinade.

In saucepan, bring marinade to boil, and set aside. Preheat oven to 425 degrees. Rub tenderloin with ground black pepper, and place on rack in roasting pan. Arrange bacon on top, and roast 45–50 minutes, until thermometer registers 135 degrees, basting occasionally with marinade. Spoon chutney over tenderloin, and roast for 5–10 minutes longer, until thermometer reads 145 degrees for medium rare and 160 degrees for medium. Remove to meat platter, and let rest 10 minutes before slicing.
Yield: 8–10 servings

BEEF TENDERLOIN WITH SPICY CRAWFISH SAUCE

The Crawfish Sauce is also great as a dip.

6 beef tenderloins (tenderloin may be left whole or
    sliced into filets)
1 (16-ounce) bottle Dale's Steak Seasoning
3 (12-ounce) packages frozen crawfish tails
½ cup butter, divided
1 cup sliced green onions
1 cup chopped sweet red bell peppers
12 ounces cream cheese
4 cloves garlic, minced
1 tablespoon crushed red pepper flakes
1 teaspoon freshly ground black pepper
Salt to taste
¼ cup half-and-half

While tenderloin is marinating in Dale's, rinse crawfish tails in cool water and drain. In a large nonstick skillet, sauté crawfish in 2 tablespoons butter for 5–10 minutes or until tender; remove and set aside. Add remaining butter to pan and sauté onions and peppers in butter until tender. Stir in cream cheese, garlic, red pepper flakes, black pepper, and salt. When cream cheese has melted and mixture is smooth, add crawfish and half-and-half and heat thoroughly. Cover and remove from heat. Cook steaks on grill. After steaks are cooked, reheat crawfish mixture and pour over steaks.
Yield: 6 servings

Oven Filets of Beef

OVEN FILETS OF BEEF

1 tablespoon seasoned salt
½ tablespoon black pepper
16 (6- to 8-ounce) filet mignons, 1-inch thick
1 stick plus 2 tablespoons butter, divided
2 tablespoons brandy
3 tablespoons all-purpose flour
2 teaspoons tomato paste
1 teaspoon crushed garlic
¾ cup dry red wine
2 cups chicken broth
½ cup beef broth
½ cup water
½ teaspoon Worcestershire sauce
2 tablespoons currant jelly
½ pound fresh mushrooms, sliced

Rub seasoned salt and pepper on both sides of filets. In heavy nonstick skillet over medium-high heat, sauté filets in 2 tablespoons butter until brown on sides, but raw in the center. Divide filets between 2 (9x13-inch) casseroles.

Deglaze pan drippings with brandy over medium heat, stirring constantly, and scraping bottom of pan. Add remaining butter. When melted, stir in flour. Reduce heat to low and cook, stirring constantly, until mixture is golden. Stir in tomato paste and garlic (mixture will be thick and grainy). Remove pan from heat and whisk in wine, chicken broth, beef broth, and water. Return to medium heat and bring to a boil, stirring constantly. Reduce heat and simmer, stirring occasionally for 10 minutes or until reduced by a third. Stir in Worcestershire and currant jelly. When jelly melts, stir in mushrooms. Sauce should be coating consistency. If too thick, thin with water. Cool completely. Divide sauce, and pour half over steaks in each casserole. Cover casseroles with foil and chill overnight. Bring to room temperature. Preheat oven to 400 degrees. Bake uncovered for 15–20 minutes for medium rare, 20–25 minutes for medium to medium-well done. Serve filets with sauce.
Yield: 16 servings

ITALIAN BEEF

1 (4- to 5-pound) rump roast
1 cup Worcestershire sauce
1 tablespoon parsley flakes
2 teaspoons basil
1 tablespoon Italian seasoning
2 teaspoons oregano
2 teaspoons Tabasco sauce
½ cup water
½ cup each: mayonnaise and sour cream
2 tablespoons Zatarain's Creole Mustard

Preheat oven to 450 degrees. Place roast in baking pan and pour Worcestershire over roast. Sprinkle with parsley, basil, Italian seasoning, and oregano. Sprinkle with Tabasco. Cover and bake 15 minutes. Reduce heat to 250 degrees and bake for 5 hours. Remove from oven and slice into pieces. Add ½ cup water, cover, and return to oven for 1 hour. For sauce, combine mayonnaise, sour cream, and mustard.
Yield: 8–10 servings

CONFECTIONERS' SUGAR RIB-EYE STEAKS

The sugar gives these steaks a nice crust.

4 (4- to 6-ounce) rib-eye steaks
½ cup Worcestershire sauce
1 tablespoon soy sauce
1 teaspoon Lawry's Seasoned Salt
Black pepper and garlic powder to taste
½ cup confectioners' sugar

Marinate steaks for 2 hours in a mixture of Worcestershire sauce and soy sauce. Remove steaks and sprinkle with seasoned salt, pepper, and garlic powder; rub into both sides of meat. Cover surface of steaks with confectioners' sugar, and rub into both sides. Cook on a grill to desired doneness. Do not pierce or the juices and seasonings will escape.
Yield: 4 servings

Italian Beef

CROCKPOT ROAST

1 (.87-ounce) package dry brown gravy mix
2 (10¾-ounce) cans cream of mushroom soup
1 (3- to 4-pound) chuck roast
Worcestershire sauce to taste
1 onion, chopped
1 bell pepper, chopped
1 (8-ounce) jar sliced mushrooms
Salt and black pepper to taste
½ cup Italian salad dressing

Mix gravy mix and 1 can soup in crockpot. Add roast and top with second can of soup. Drizzle with Worcestershire. Add onion, bell pepper, mushrooms, salt, and pepper. Pour dressing over all ingredients. Cover, and cook on HIGH for 4 hours. Serve over rice or potatoes.
Yield: 8–10 servings

GOURMET MEATLOAF

1 pound ground round
1 cup soft fresh bread crumbs
½ cup chopped fresh basil
½ cup oil-packed sun-dried tomatoes, chopped
½ cup finely chopped onion
½ cup shredded Provolone cheese
2 eggs, beaten
1 garlic clove, chopped
⅓ cup ketchup

Preheat oven to 350 degrees. Line a 5x9-inch loaf pan with foil. Combine all but ketchup in bowl, and mix well. Spoon into loaf pan, and top with ketchup. Bake for one hour.
Yield: 8–10 servings

STUFFED BELL PEPPERS

4 large bell peppers, any color
¾ pound ground chuck
1 onion, chopped
2 cloves garlic, minced
2 teaspoons beef bouillon granules, divided
½ teaspoon salt
½ teaspoon black pepper
1 teaspoon garlic powder
1 cup cooked rice
½ cup shredded Cheddar cheese
¼ cup salsa
1 Roma tomato, diced
1 tablespoon soy sauce
1 cup hot water

Preheat oven to 350 degrees. Cut pepper in half lengthwise. Remove the seeds and ribs. Sauté the beef, onion, garlic, 1 teaspoon of bouillon granules, salt, pepper, and garlic powder together until beef is browned. Drain fat. Add rice, cheese, salsa, tomato, and soy sauce. Mix well and stuff the mixture into the peppers. In a small bowl, mix the hot water and remaining bouillon granules. Pour this mixture into a casserole dish large enough to hold all of the peppers. Place the peppers in the dish, cover with foil, and bake for 25–30 minutes. Remove foil and spoon the juice from the bottom of the pan on top of the peppers. Bake an additional 10 minutes.
Yield: 4 servings

Crockpot Roast

MARINATED BEEF KABOBS

These kabobs are just perfect with rice or potatoes.

¾ cup Allegro Original Marinade

¾ cup Worcestershire sauce

½ cup low-sodium soy sauce

½ cup honey

1 teaspoon ground ginger

¼ cup Weber Chicago Steak Seasoning, divided

3 pounds sirloin, rib-eye, or filet, cut into cubes

1½ pounds link sausage, cut into ½-inch round slices

1 pound bacon, cut into 2-inch pieces

3 large onions, cut into pieces and pulled apart

Bell peppers, squash, zucchini, onions, and tomatoes

Olive oil

Greek seasoning

For marinade, mix Allegro, Worcestershire, soy sauce, honey, ginger, and 2 tablespoons steak seasoning. Marinate steaks in zipper bag in refrigerator 8–24 hours. Grill sausage on medium heat about 15 minutes until half done. Remove, and cool. On wooden skewers, alternate steak, bacon, sausage, and onion. Sprinkle with remaining steak seasoning to taste. Alternate vegetables on separate skewers, brush with olive oil, and sprinkle with Greek seasoning. Grill steak kabobs on medium-heat 25–40 minutes, to desired doneness. Grill vegetable kabobs separately. To serve with rare steak, place vegetables on grill 5–10 minutes before meat. For medium to well-done steak, place meat kabobs and vegetable kabobs on grill at the same time. Serve over rice.

Yield: 6–8 servings

TARTE FLAMBE

DOUGH:

1 small package yeast
1 teaspoon sugar
1⅓ cups room-temperature water, divided
1 tablespoon fine sea salt
2 cups all-purpose flour

Mix yeast, sugar, and 1 cup lukewarm water in a bowl. Stir until dissolved; cover with a cloth for 15 minutes. Mix remaining water with salt; set aside. Gradually add flour to yeast mixture; mix for 2–3 minutes. Knead Dough on low speed with a mixer; slowly add saltwater. Dough must not stick to bowl; it must be firm and slightly sticky. Place Dough on a floured surface, and knead for a minute. Cover with a cloth; let rise for 40 minutes. When it has risen, flatten Dough with your hands for a minute. Cover with a cloth; let rise 40 minutes. Flatten Dough, and knead 2–3 minutes.

FILLING:

1 large yellow onion, finely minced
2 tablespoons vegetable oil, divided
2 pinches salt, divided
1 (8-ounce) carton sour cream
2 egg yolks
Pinch of nutmeg and black pepper
1 cup chopped smoked ham or bacon
Grated Gruyère cheese

Preheat oven to 400 degrees. Sauté onion in 1 tablespoon oil and 1 pinch salt for 5 minutes, until transparent. Mix sour cream and egg yolks with a fork. Season with nutmeg, 1 pinch salt, and pepper. Add onion, and mix. With rolling pin, spread Dough thinly in a circular shape. Lay Dough on an oiled baking sheet without an edge. Spread Filling on Dough, and sprinkle with ham and cheese. Pour remaining oil on top, and bake 10–15 minutes or until golden brown.
Yield: 6 servings

PORTOBELLO PESTO BACON PIZZA WITH ARTICHOKES AND PARMESAN

These pizzas are also great as appetizers or as a side.

4 large portobello mushroom caps, wiped clean
1 tablespoon olive oil
Salt and black pepper to taste
4 slices bacon
3 tablespoons pesto sauce
1 (8-ounce) package cream cheese, softened
¼ cup canned artichokes, drained and chopped
4 tablespoons freshly grated Parmesan cheese

Brush both sides of mushrooms with 1 tablespoon oil; sprinkle lightly with salt and pepper, and place on a preheated grill. Grill for 4 minutes on each side over medium heat. Fry bacon until crisp. Drain and crumble. Stir pesto and cream cheese together until blended. Spread the cool portobellos with the pesto/cream cheese spread, and top with bacon and artichokes. Sprinkle 1 tablespoon Parmesan cheese on top of each pesto portobello. Return to grill on medium-low heat, and cover. Grill until topping is hot, 6–10 minutes.
Yield: 4 servings

 BIG RIVER TENDERLOIN

This creamy sauce is wonderful!

¼ cup chopped green onions
¼ cup chopped parsley
2 cloves garlic, chopped
½ stick butter
½ pound shrimp, peeled and deveined
Salt and black and ground red pepper to taste
1 (2-pound) pork tenderloin
Tony Chachere's Creole Seasoning to taste

Sauté onions, parsley, and garlic in butter. Add shrimp, and cook until done. Season with salt and peppers, and cool. Stuff pork tenderloin with shrimp mixture, and season with Creole seasoning. Grill for one hour or until cooked through.
Yield: 6–8 servings

SAUCE:

¼ cup each: chopped onion and parsley
2 cloves garlic, chopped
1 stick butter
2 tablespoons flour
1 pound shrimp, peeled and deveined
1 pint half-and-half
Worcestershire sauce and thyme to taste
Salt and black and ground red pepper to taste

Sauté onions, parsley, and garlic in butter. Add flour, and mix. Add shrimp, and heat. Add half-and-half, Worcestershire, and thyme. Thin with water, if too thick. Cook for 10–15 minutes; season with salt and peppers. Pour over sliced tenderloin when ready to serve.

STUFFED PORK TENDERLOIN

½ cup chopped onion
¼ cup butter
½ cup chopped carrots
1 small bunch spinach leaves
1 cup dried cranberries
⅓ cup toasted pine nuts
1 (2-pound) pork tenderloin
½ pound lean bacon
½ teaspoon each: onion powder and garlic powder
1 (8-ounce) jar apricot preserves

Preheat oven to 350 degrees. In saucepan, sauté onions in butter until soft; add carrots. Add spinach and sauté until wilted. Remove from heat, and stir in cranberries and pine nuts; cool. Butterfly tenderloin and pound to ½-inch thick. Place in 9x13-inch baking dish lined with enough foil to wrap around stuffed pork. Lay bacon strips across dish and one strip on each end. Place tenderloin on bacon, season with onion and garlic powders, and place stuffing on top. Fold the tenderloin together and season with onion and garlic powders. Braid bacon around the pork. Seal foil loosely around tenderloin. Bake for about 1½ hours. Open foil, pour off fat, and turn oven up to 450 degrees. Heat for 10 minutes or until bacon is brown. Coat tenderloin with preserves, and heat 5–10 minutes longer.
Yield: 6–8 servings

 THE BEST PORK TENDERLOIN

2 (6½-ounce) pork tenderloins
Salt and black pepper to taste
1 cup orange juice
½ cup soy sauce
¼ cup olive oil
2 tablespoons chopped fresh rosemary

Sprinkle both sides of tenderloins with salt and pepper. Combine remaining ingredients and pour over pork in a 9x13-inch glass baking dish. Marinate in refrigerator for 2 hours. Remove and bake in a preheated 400-degree oven for 20–25 minutes. Let rest 10–15 minutes. Slice and serve with pan sauce.
Yield: 10–12 servings

PORK LOIN AND POTATOES

4 red potatoes, peeled and cubed
3 sweet potatoes, peeled and cubed
1 green apple, cubed
2 tablespoons olive oil
1 tablespoon ground cinnamon
1 (2- to 3-pound) boneless pork loin roast
5 tablespoons butter, sliced
Salt and black pepper to taste
1 (8-ounce) bottle Dr. Pete's Praline Mustard Glaze

Preheat oven to 375 degrees. Place potatoes and apple in a large zipper bag. Add olive oil and cinnamon. Shake bag to coat. Place roast in a buttered baking dish. Arrange potato mixture around the roast. Top the roast with butter slices, and salt and pepper. Cover with foil and bake for 1 hour and 15 minutes. Remove foil and bake for 15 minutes. Cool roast slightly, and slice. Pour Dr. Pete's glaze over pork.
Yield: 6–8 servings

MAPLE GLAZED HAM

This ham is sweet and flavorful.

1 (10- to 12-pound) fresh ham
Salt and black pepper to taste
1 (16-ounce) can sliced pineapple
1 (8-ounce) jar maraschino cherries
1 tablespoon whole cloves
1 cup brown sugar
½ cup each: prepared mustard and maple syrup

Preheat oven to 400 degrees. Sprinkle ham with salt and pepper. With knife, score ham in a diamond pattern. Place pineapple slices and cherries on ham and secure with cloves. Roast uncovered for 30 minutes. Decrease oven temperature to 300 degrees, and roast for 18–20 minutes per pound. Combine brown sugar, mustard, and maple syrup. Spread over ham for last 45 minutes of baking. Baste and bake until meat thermometer reads 160 degrees. Remove from oven, cover loosely with foil, and let rest 20 minutes before slicing.
Yield: 20–24 servings

CHIPOTLE-MAPLE BARBEQUED PORK CHOPS WITH SWEET TANGERINE-BLACKBERRY SALSA

4 (2-inch-thick) center-cut loin pork chops
1 teaspoon all-purpose seasoning
2 cloves garlic, minced
1 cup bottled barbeque sauce
¼ cup maple syrup
2 teaspoons fresh lime juice
1 teaspoon freshly grated lime zest
1 chipotle in adobo sauce (from a 5-ounce can), minced
½ teaspoon adobo sauce

Brush grill with oil, and heat to medium. Rub pork chops with seasoning; set aside. In 2½-quart saucepan, combine garlic, barbeque sauce, maple syrup, lime juice, lime zest, chipotle pepper, and adobo sauce. Bring to a simmer, and cook for 2 minutes, stirring occasionally. Remove from heat, and transfer to a bowl. Set aside. Grill chops for 10 minutes per side, turning occasionally, and brushing with chipotle barbeque sauce mixture during the last 4 minutes of grilling. Remove from grill, and let chops rest for about 5 minutes. Serve with Sweet Tangerine-Blackberry Salsa.
Yield: 4 servings

SWEET TANGERINE-BLACKBERRY SALSA:
½ cup frozen sweetened blackberries, defrosted
2 teaspoons fresh tangerine juice
1 teaspoon freshly grated tangerine zest
1 teaspoon seedless blackberry jam
½ teaspoon sea salt
½ cup diced sweet onion
½ cup peeled, seeded, and diced cucumber
½ cup fresh blackberries

Combine defrosted blackberries, tangerine juice, zest, and jam. Bring to a simmer, stirring occasionally for 4 minutes, then stir in salt, onion, cucumber, and fresh blackberries.

JALAPEÑO-BASIL PORK CHOPS

1 (10-ounce) jar red jalapeño pepper jelly
½ cup dry white wine
¼ cup chopped fresh basil
4 (1½-inch-thick) bone-in loin chops, well
 trimmed
4 small slices smoked Gouda cheese
½ teaspoon salt
¼ teaspoon black pepper
For garnish: green onions

In a small saucepan over low heat, combine jelly, wine, and basil, whisking for about 5 minutes or until pepper jelly melts. Remove from heat, and let mixture cool completely. Cut a pocket into loin side of chop, large enough to insert and hold cheese, and insert cheese as close to bone as possible; avoid too large of a piece to prevent melting during cooking. Skewer pocket closed.

Pour ¾ cup pepper jelly mixture into a large zipper freezer bag and reserve remaining ¼ cup mixture; add pork chops, turning to coat. Seal and let marinate for 1½–2 hours in refrigerator. Allow chops to come to room temperature for 30 minutes before grilling, turning pork chops occasionally. Remove chops from marinade. Discard marinade. Sprinkle chops evenly with salt and pepper. Grill, covered, over high heat (425 degrees) for 3 minutes, then turn a quarter turn and cook another 3 minutes, then repeat on the other side, or until a meat thermometer inserted into thickest portion registers 145 degrees (temperature should rise another 10 degrees at rest). Strain reserved ¼ cup marinade, and boil 2 minutes. Garnish pork chops with pepper jelly mixture and green onions.
Yield: 4 servings

Roasted Chicken and Potatoes

POULTRY

ROASTED CHICKEN AND POTATOES

16 new potatoes, not peeled
1 teaspoon thyme
4 tablespoons olive oil, divided
4 chicken breasts
Salt and ground black pepper to taste
½ teaspoon garlic powder
Juice and zest of 1 lemon
8 slices bacon
½ cup white wine
1 green onion, sliced
2 tablespoons heavy cream

Boil potatoes until slightly tender; drain and sprinkle with thyme and 2 tablespoons oil. Preheat oven to 425 degrees. Rub chicken breasts with remaining oil and season with salt, pepper, garlic powder, lemon juice, and zest. Place chicken and potatoes in a foil-lined, greased baking pan, and bake for 20 minutes. Remove, and wrap 2 bacon slices around each breast, and return for 20 minutes until crisp. Remove chicken and potatoes. For gravy, transfer drippings to a saucepan. Heat over medium heat; add wine and onion and heat for 3 minutes. Whisk in cream; stir for 2 minutes or until thickened.
Yield: 4 servings

PARMESAN CHICKEN

¾ cup grated Parmesan cheese
¾ cup Italian bread crumbs
1 (3½-ounce) can French fried onions, crushed
2 teaspoons garlic salt
6 boneless, skinless chicken breasts
1 stick margarine, melted

Preheat oven to 350 degrees. Combine cheese, bread crumbs, onions, and garlic salt. Roll chicken in margarine, then in dry ingredients. Place in greased casserole dish, cover in foil, and bake 45 minutes. Remove foil and bake an additional 15 minutes.
Yield: 6 servings

CHICKEN WITH BACON AND ROSEMARY

These individual servings make a beautiful presentation with fresh rosemary.

4 boneless, skinless chicken breasts
Salt and ground black pepper to taste
16 thin bacon strips
4 sprigs fresh rosemary
2 tablespoons olive oil
For garnish: fresh rosemary

Season each chicken breast with salt and pepper. Roll each breast in 4 bacon strips into a tight cylinder shape. Sprinkle with rosemary. Wrap each in plastic wrap, twisting ends tightly. Chill overnight.

Preheat oven to 300 degrees. Heat a skillet, and add oil. Unwrap breasts, and place in hot oil. Brown bacon on all sides. Remove from skillet, and place in a foil-lined baking dish; bake for 10–15 minutes. Remove from oven and let rest for 3 minutes before slicing into thick disks.
Yield: 4 servings

BAKED LEMON CHICKEN

¼ cup dry bread crumbs
2 tablespoons grated Parmesan cheese
1 teaspoon dried parsley flakes (2 tablespoons fresh)
2 boneless, skinless chicken breasts
½ stick margarine, melted
1 tablespoon fresh lemon juice

Preheat oven to 350 degrees. Pat chicken dry. Mix bread crumbs, cheese, and parsley. Dip chicken in crumb mixture, coating both sides, and place in a greased glass baking dish. Melt butter; stir in lemon juice. Pour over chicken. Bake for 35 minutes.
Yield: 2 servings

Chicken with
Bacon and Rosemary

CAJUN CHICKEN LASAGNA

This lasagna is so creamy and spicy.

16 lasagna noodles, cooked al dente

1 tablespoon olive oil

1 pound andouille sausage, quartered lengthwise and sliced

8 boneless, skinless chicken breasts, cut into bite-sized pieces

3 teaspoons Cajun seasoning

1 (12-ounce) package frozen seasoning blend (onions, celery, bell peppers, parsley)

2 (15-ounce) jars Alfredo sauce, divided

1 (2-ounce) package grated Parmesan cheese

1 (8-ounce) package shredded mozzarella cheese, divided

Preheat oven to 325 degrees. Combine cooked noodles with olive oil; set aside. Combine sausage, chicken, and Cajun seasoning. In a large skillet, cook meat about 8 minutes. Remove meat from skillet, reserving drippings. Add seasoning blend and sauté until tender. Remove from heat, and stir in meat, 1 jar sauce, and Parmesan cheese. Arrange 4 noodles on bottom a greased 9x13-inch baking dish, and spread with a third of the meat mixture. Sprinkle with ½ cup mozzarella cheese. Repeat layers twice, ending with 4 noodles. Spread remaining Alfredo sauce over top. Cover with foil, and bake 1 hour. Let stand 15 minutes before serving.

Yield: 12–16 servings

SIDNEY'S CHICKEN CROQUETTES

6 tablespoons butter
½ cup all-purpose flour
1 cup milk
1 cup chicken broth
2 tablespoons each: minced parsley, lemon juice,
    and grated onion
½ teaspoon salt
1 hen, cooked, meat removed and finely chopped
2 eggs, beaten
2 cups saltine cracker crumbs
Dash of black pepper and paprika

Melt butter; blend in flour, milk, and broth. Stir until smooth. Add parsley, lemon juice, onion, and salt. Cook until thick; cool. Add meat; chill. With wet hands, shape chicken mixture into 3-inch tall pyramid shapes, and roll in crumbs mixed with pepper and paprika. Dip into beaten eggs and roll in crumb mixture again. Fry in hot oil until golden brown; drain. Serve with Lemon Cream Sauce. May be made the day before. (After browning croquettes, chill, and bake at 350 degrees for 30 minutes.)
Yield: 1 dozen

LEMON CREAM SAUCE:

4 tablespoons butter
4 tablespoons all-purpose flour
1 cup each: chicken broth and milk
4 egg yolks, beaten
1 tablespoon each: chopped pimientos and parsley
4 tablespoons lemon juice

Melt butter and stir in flour, making a smooth paste. Add broth and milk. When hot, add a small amount of the liquid to the egg yolks, then add the yolks back to the sauce. When thickened, add pimientos, parsley, and lemon juice.

CHICKEN AND PASTA IN CREAM SAUCE

8 boneless, skinless chicken breasts
Seasoned salt and black pepper to taste
1½ sticks butter, divided
1 (16-ounce) package angel hair pasta, cooked
1 (8-ounce) package cream cheese
1 cup grated Parmesan cheese
2 cups half-and-half
6 slices bacon
3 green onions, chopped with white bulbs
2 cups sliced mushrooms

Preheat oven to 350 degrees. Season chicken with salt and pepper. Place in a foil-lined pan with pat of butter on each breast. Cover; bake 30 minutes. Over low heat, melt cream cheese, Parmesan cheese, 1 stick butter, and half-and-half; set aside. In skillet, cook bacon; drain and crumble. In drippings, sauté onions and mushrooms 10 minutes. Stir in cream cheese mixture and bacon. Serve sauce over pasta and chicken.
Yield: 8 servings

PARMESAN CHICKEN PASTA

1 (12-ounce) box bow tie pasta, cooked al dente
3 boneless, skinless chicken breasts, cut into bite-
    sized pieces
¼ teaspoon garlic powder
1 teaspoon Tony Chachere's Creole seasoning
Salt and black pepper to taste
2 tablespoons olive oil
1½ cups mayonnaise
1½ cups shredded Parmesan cheese, divided

Season chicken with garlic powder, Creole seasoning, salt and pepper. Sauté chicken in olive oil for 10 minutes; set aside. Preheat oven to 325 degrees. Combine mayonnaise and 1 cup cheese, and stir into pasta. Add chicken. Pour into a greased 2-quart baking dish, and sprinkle with remaining cheese. Bake 30 minutes.
Yield: 8 servings

CHICKEN AND DUMPLINGS

This is my mother's recipe that brings back sweet memories.

4 chicken breasts, bone in and skin on
4 ribs celery, halved
1 onion, quartered
Salt and black pepper to taste
2 cups all-purpose flour
½ cup shortening
1 egg, beaten
¾–1 cup water
3 tablespoons margarine, divided

Bring pot of water to a boil. Add chicken breasts, celery, onion, salt, and pepper. Reduce heat to medium-low heat, and simmer for 30 minutes. Cover and let stand for 30 minutes. Remove chicken to cool, discard vegetables, and reserve stock. Remove chicken from bones, and chop into bite-sized pieces; place in a 2-quart baking dish and set aside. In a bowl, mix flour, ½ teaspoon salt, shortening, and egg together. Add water and mix well. On a floured surface, roll out half of dough to about ¼ inch thick. With a knife, cut into 1x3-inch dumplings. Drop a few dumplings at a time into boiling broth. Do not stir; use a fork to separate dumplings. Boil for 5 minutes, remove dumplings and place over chicken. Cook all dumplings and place over chicken. Add 1 tablespoon margarine to broth. Pour broth over chicken and dumplings to cover. Preheat oven to 400 degrees. Roll out remaining half of dough, and place over top of filling. Dot with remaining margarine. Bake for 30 minutes until golden brown.
Yield: 8–10 servings

ROLLED CHICKEN BREASTS

1 (2¼-ounce) jar sliced, dried beef
6 boneless, skinless chicken breasts
White pepper, paprika, onion salt, and celery salt to taste
12 bacon strips
2 (10¾-ounce) cans cream of mushroom soup
1 cup sour cream
1 (8-ounce) package cream cheese, softened
Cooked rice

Preheat oven to 275 degrees. Spread dried beef in a single layer on the bottom of a greased 9x13-inch baking dish. Cut each breast into 2 flat, thin pieces. Sprinkle each piece with pepper, paprika, onion salt, and celery salt. Roll up each piece with spices on the inside; wrap with a piece of bacon, and secure with a toothpick. Place each chicken roll on top of a piece of dried beef. Combine soup, sour cream, and cream cheese; pour over chicken. Cover with foil, and bake for 2½ hours. Remove foil and brown for 20 minutes. Serve over rice.
Yield: 6–8 servings

CHICKEN AND RICE CASSEROLE

2 cups cooked and diced chicken
1 (10¾-ounce) can cream of chicken soup
¾ cup mayonnaise
1 cup cooked rice
1 tablespoon lemon juice
1 stick butter, melted
1 stack buttery crackers, crushed

Preheat oven to 350 degrees. Combine chicken, soup, mayonnaise, rice, and lemon juice. Pour into a greased 1½-quart baking dish. Combine butter and cracker crumbs, and sprinkle over casserole. Bake 30 minutes.
Yield: 8 servings

CHICKEN POT PIE

This is the ultimate comfort food.

4 chicken breasts, bone in and skin on
2 carrots, peeled
4 ribs celery, halved
1 onion, quartered
½ stick butter
½ cup all-purpose flour
2 cups plus 2 tablespoons heavy cream, divided
Milk to thin
Salt, black pepper, and Tabasco sauce to taste
1 (15-ounce) package rolled pie crusts
1 egg yolk

Boil chicken, carrots, celery, onion, salt, and pepper. Reduce heat, and simmer 30 minutes. Cover, and let stand 30 minutes. Remove chicken and vegetables to cool, reserving stock. Debone chicken, and chop vegetables; set aside. Preheat oven to 400 degrees. In a saucepan, melt butter and whisk in flour to form a paste. Gradually stir in one cup chicken stock and 2 cups cream. Thin with milk. Add chicken, vegetables, and seasonings. Pour into greased 2-quart baking dish. Place crust on top and pinch edges. Decorate with remaining dough. Brush crust with a glaze of egg yolk beaten with remaining 2 tablespoons cream. Bake 30–45 minutes until crust is golden. Yield: 8–10 servings

ROAST TURKEY

BRINE:
2 gallons cold water, divided
1 cup kosher salt
1 cup sugar
1 brining bag

Boil 2 quarts water, add salt and sugar, and stir until dissolved. Add remaining water, and cool. Remove neck and giblets from turkey. Place turkey and brine into bag, seal tightly, and place on the lowest shelf of the refrigerator for 12–24 hours, turning occasionally. Remove turkey from bag, pat dry, and roast turkey.
Yield: 2 gallons Brine

1 (16- to 18-pound) brined turkey
Fresh sage leaves
1 cup olive oil, divided
Salt and ground black pepper to taste
Cheesecloth

Preheat oven to 350 degrees. Loosen skin around breast of brined turkey, and place sage under skin. Rub bird with half of oil, salt, and pepper. Wrap in cheesecloth, and pour remaining oil over bird. Place turkey, breast side up, on rack in roasting pan, and cover loosely with foil. Roast for 12 minutes per pound, and remove foil for last hour of cooking. Insert an instant-read thermometer into the thickest part of the thigh not touching bone, and turkey is done when temperature registers 185 degrees and juices are clear. Remove cheesecloth, and let turkey rest for 20 minutes before carving.
Yield: 24–30 servings

ROASTED TURKEY WITH CITRUS-ROSEMARY SALT

CITRUS-ROSEMARY SALT:
½ tablespoon chopped fresh rosemary leaves
2 tablespoons lemon zest
¼ cup coarse salt

In food processor, pulse rosemary leaves, lemon zest, and salt. Store in an airtight container for 24 hours.

1 (8- to 10-pound) turkey
½ cup olive oil, divided
1 long sprig fresh rosemary
1 lemon, halved
2 carrots
4 ribs celery

Preheat oven to 425 degrees. Remove necks and giblets from turkey; wash and dry turkey. Rub turkey inside and out with ¼ cup oil, and season outside with Citrus-Rosemary Salt. Place rosemary sprig and lemon halves inside cavity of bird. Place turkey on top of carrots and celery ribs on a foil-lined baking sheet. Drizzle with remaining ¼ cup oil. Bake, uncovered, for 2–2½ hours. Remove from pan, and let rest for 15 minutes before slicing.
Yield: 12–16 servings

SMOKED TURKEY BREAST

½ cup honey
¼ cup sherry or apple cider
Juice of 1 lemon
3 tablespoons butter
2 teaspoons salt
1 (3- to 3½-pound) turkey

In a saucepan, heat honey, sherry or cider, lemon juice, butter, and salt until butter melts. Wash turkey and pat dry; marinate in honey mixture in a zipper bag for up to 24 hours. Remove from bag; discard marinade. Prepare smoker with wood chips that have been soaked in water. When chips begin to smoke and temperature reaches 250 degrees, place turkey on rack and close lid. Smoke 3–4 hours or until temperature reaches 170 degrees. Let rest for 10 minutes before slicing.
Yield: 10–12 servings

TURKEY IN A SACK

1 (12- to 16-pound) turkey, thawed
Oil
Seasoned salt to taste
1 onion, quartered
3 ribs celery, halved
2 carrots, chopped
Ground black pepper to taste
4 strips bacon
1 brown paper grocery sack

Preheat oven to 350 degrees. Remove neck and giblets from turkey; rinse, and dry. Rub cavity with oil and sprinkle with seasoned salt. Stuff with vegetables. Rub additional oil on outside of bird and coat with seasoned salt and pepper. Crisscross bacon strips over bird. Place inside brown paper sack, roll ends, and staple closed. Place in a large roasting pan, and bake for 10 minutes per pound, plus 10 minutes for large bird. When done, remove from sack, and cool for 30 minutes before slicing.
Yield: 20–24 servings

Smoked Turkey Breast

Glazed Cornish Game Hens

CORNISH HENS WITH WILD RICE PILAF

WILD RICE PILAF:

4 cups water

2 teaspoons salt

1 cup wild rice, rinsed in cold water

1 cup brown rice

2 sticks butter

1½ cups finely chopped onions

1½ cups finely chopped green bell peppers

1 (14-ounce) can chopped mushrooms, drained

1 (2-ounce) jar chopped pimientos, drained

1 teaspoon crushed dried thyme

½ cup craisins

Salt and black pepper to taste

In a saucepan, combine water and salt, and bring to a boil. Add rice, and return to a boil. Reduce heat, cover, and simmer for 20 minutes. Drain, and set aside. Preheat oven to 325 degrees. In a skillet over medium-high heat, melt butter. Sauté onions and peppers for 3 minutes. Stir in mushrooms, pimientos, and thyme; cook 4 minutes or until tender. Remove from heat; stir in rice and craisins, and season with salt and pepper.
Yield: 8 servings

4 Cornish hens

Salt and black pepper to taste

4 slices bacon

Preheat oven to 325 degrees. Season hens inside and out with salt and pepper. Stuff with Wild Rice Pilaf, and place a bacon slice on top of each hen. Bake, uncovered, for 1½–2 hours, basting with pan drippings. If hens are not tender after 1½ hours, cover and steam for the final 30 minutes. Serve with additional rice.
Yield: 4 hens

GLAZED CORNISH GAME HENS

6 Cornish hens, thawed, rinsed, and dried
Olive oil
Salt and black pepper to taste

Preheat oven to 375 degrees. Rub hens with oil and season with salt and pepper. Place breast side up in a large oiled roasting pan; roast for 30 minutes. Remove hens from oven, brush with Glaze, and bake for 40 additional minutes, basting with more Glaze every 10 minutes. Let rest 10 minutes before serving.
Yield: 6 hens

GLAZE:

½ cup chili sauce

½ cup apricot jam

¼ cup honey

1 tablespoon bourbon

2 tablespoons Worcestershire sauce

1 teaspoon garlic powder

1 teaspoon crushed rosemary

Combine ingredients.

QUAIL CASSEROLE

8–10 quail
Salt, black pepper, and poultry seasoning to taste
1 cup self-rising flour
1 cup oil
1 stick butter
8 ounces fresh mushrooms, sliced
1 onion, chopped
½ cup Madeira wine, divided
1 cup cream

Debone quail; season with salt, pepper, and poultry seasoning. Roll in flour, and brown in oil in sauté pan. Remove quail from pan, and drain excess oil. Add butter, mushrooms, and onion; brown. Add ¼ cup wine; reduce heat, and simmer. Remove mushrooms and onion; drain liquid. Add remaining ¼ cup wine, and bring to a boil. Add cream, and let thicken. Preheat oven to 375 degrees. In a greased 9x13-inch baking dish, alternate layers of quail and mushroom mixture. Pour about ¾ of the sauce over casserole. Cover, and bake for one hour. Serve with rice and remaining sauce.
Yield: 12 servings

SEARED DUCK BREAST WITH MUSTARD SAUCE

MUSTARD SAUCE:
2 shallots, diced
1 clove garlic, diced
2 tablespoons butter
½ cup red wine (drinking quality)
1 cup Kahlúa
1¼ cups Veal demi-glace
¼–½ cup Dijon mustard

Sauté shallots and garlic in butter; deglaze pan with red wine. Add Kahlúa and reduce by half; add demi-glace and again reduce by half. Strain for a smooth sauce. Return to low heat and add ¼ cup mustard. Taste; add additional mustard, if desired.

6 duck breasts
Salt to taste

Preheat oven to 350 degrees. Score fat side of each duck breast with 3 or 4 slits; salt to taste, and place fat side down in an oven-ready skillet. Sear duck on medium-high heat 6–8 minutes until fat side is crisp. Transfer skillet to oven and bake 10 minutes until medium-rare. Remove from oven, and allow to rest 10 minutes before slicing. Serve with Mustard Sauce.
Yield: 6 servings

GRILLED CINNAMON DUCK

1 cup butter, melted
2 tablespoons ground cinnamon
Salt and black pepper to taste
4 duck breasts

Mix together butter, cinnamon, salt, and pepper; pour half of mixture over duck breasts to cover in a large bowl. Reserve remaining butter mixture. Marinate overnight. Grill over a medium fire for about 6 minutes on each side, basting with remaining butter mixture. Slice and sprinkle with additional cinnamon.
Yield: 4 servings

APPLE SPICED DUCKLING

1½ cups apple juice
¾ cup apple cider vinegar
¾ cup brown sugar
¾ cup maple syrup
1 (4- to 5-pound) duckling, thawed
Salt and black pepper to taste
Butcher's string (for tying legs)

In a saucepan over medium-high heat, combine juice, vinegar, brown sugar, and maple syrup; reduce by half. Remove neck and giblets from cavity of duck. Trim neck and tail fat close to bird. Score skin with sharp knife, being careful not to puncture flesh. Season duck inside the cavity and out with salt and pepper.

Preheat oven to 450 degrees. Place duck, breast side up, on a rack in a roasting pan, tucking wings back and tying legs. Bake for 25 minutes without opening the door. Lower temperature to 350 degrees, and coat duck with half of glaze, reserving half. Continue to cook for another 25 minutes (50 minutes total cooking time). Pour on a final glaze once duck is removed from the oven, and allow bird to cool 15 minutes before carving.
Yield: 6–8 servings

Grilled Grouper with Avocado and Tomato

SEAFOOD

GRILLED GROUPER WITH AVOCADO AND TOMATO

AVOCADO AND TOMATO RELISH:

1 avocado, cut and diced
1 small red onion, finely diced
1 tablespoon balsamic vinegar
½ teaspoon sea salt
1 large tomato, seeded and diced
½ cup peeled, seeded, and diced cucumber
1 tablespoon each: minced chives and chopped basil
2 tablespoons extra virgin olive oil

Combine avocado, onion, vinegar, and salt. Add remaining ingredients; toss. Cover and chill.

4 (6- to 7-ounce) grouper fillets
3 tablespoons extra virgin olive oil
Salt and black pepper to taste

Brush both sides of fish with olive oil. Season with salt and pepper. Grill on oiled grilling rack on high 3–4 minutes per side until browned. Reduce heat to low; grill 3–4 minutes per side. Serve with Avocado and Tomato Relish.
Yield: 4 servings

REDFISH PICCATA

2 redfish fillets
Tony Chachere's Creole seasoning
Cracked black pepper
Olive oil

Preheat oven to 450 degrees. Season fish with seasonings and olive oil. Bake 20–30 minutes in a foil-lined pan. Serve with Sauce.

SAUCE:

2 tablespoons olive oil
4 tablespoons capers
1 cup chopped heirloom tomatoes
1 tablespoon lemon juice
2 tablespoons butter

Sauté capers in olive oil for 2–3 minutes. Add tomatoes and cook another 2–3 minutes. Add lemon juice and butter; cook 2–3 minutes until heated through and pour over redfish.
Yield: 2 servings

Redfish Piccata

Grilled Tuna with Mango Salsa

SIMPLE ROASTED SALMON

This is an easy way to prepare a special entrée.

¼ cup orange juice
¼ cup fresh lemon juice
4 salmon fillets
2 tablespoons brown sugar
Zest of 1 lemon
4 teaspoons chili powder
½ teaspoon ground cumin
½ teaspoon coarse salt
½ stick butter

Combine orange juice and lemon juice in a zipper bag with fillets and marinate in refrigerator for 1–2 hours, turning several times. Discard marinade, and drain salmon on paper towels.

Preheat oven to 375 degrees. For rub, combine brown sugar, lemon zest, chili powder, cumin, and salt. Rub half of mixture over fillets. Place in a baking dish. Add remaining rub on the top side of fillets. Top each fillet with 3 very thin pats of butter. Bake for 15 minutes or until fish flakes easily with a fork.
Yield: 4 servings

GRILLED TUNA WITH MANGO SALSA

MANGO SALSA:
1 mango, chopped
1 each: tomato and red bell pepper, diced
4 green onions, chopped
½ jalapeño, minced
Juice of 2 limes
1 teaspoon each: chopped cilantro and parsley
½ teaspoon cumin
Salt and black pepper to taste

Combine ingredients and chill one hour.

2 tuna fillets
Olive oil
Juice of 2 lemons
Salt and black pepper to taste

Drizzle fillets with olive oil and lemon juice, and season with salt and pepper. Place on grill on medium-high heat. Cook 4–5 minutes per side. Serve topped with Mango Salsa.
Yield: 2 servings

Panéed Catfish with Tabasco Tartar Sauce

PANÉED CATFISH WITH TABASCO TARTAR SAUCE

4–6 catfish fillets, rinsed and patted dry
¼ cup flour, seasoned with salt and pepper
1 stick butter, cut into pieces
¼ cup olive oil

Dredge fillets in seasoned flour. Fry fillets in olive oil and butter 2–3 minutes per side until golden. Serve with Tabasco Tartar Sauce.
Yield: 6 servings

TABASCO TARTAR SAUCE:

1 cup mayonnaise
1 tablespoon each: chopped parsley, chopped chives, and capers
2 tablespoons chopped sweet pickles
1 green onion, chopped (green and white parts)
¼ teaspoon Dijon mustard
1 tablespoon Tabasco sauce
Salt, black pepper, and chopped fresh dill to taste

Combine ingredients and chill.

CREOLE CATFISH

A perfect oven-baked fish!

½ cup grated Parmesan cheese
¼ cup yellow cornmeal
½ teaspoon paprika
2 tablespoons blackened seafood seasoning
1 tablespoon Creole seasoning
¼ teaspoon garlic powder
6 catfish fillets

Preheat oven to 400 degrees. Grease foil-lined baking sheet. Combine cheese, cornmeal, and seasonings in zipper bag. Coat each fillet in dry ingredients in bag, and place on prepared baking sheet. Spray fish with nonstick spray. Place baking sheet on bottom rack of oven, and cook 20–25 minutes until golden brown and crispy.
Yield: 6 servings

CAJUN SCALLOPS WITH HONEY BUTTER SAUCE

12 large scallops
1 tablespoon Cajun seasoning
2 cups buttermilk
2 cups all-purpose flour
2 tablespoons vegetable oil
For garnish: fresh dill and lemon slices

Preheat oven to 400 degrees. Season scallops with Cajun seasoning. Place buttermilk and flour each in a dish. Dip scallops in buttermilk, then coat in flour. Heat oil in an oven-proof skillet over medium-high heat. Add scallops and cook for one minute on each side. Transfer skillet to oven and cook for one minute. Drizzle with warm Honey Butter Sauce. Garnish with dill and lemon slices.
Yield: 4 servings

HONEY BUTTER SAUCE:
⅔ cup chicken stock
3 tablespoons apple cider vinegar
1 stick butter, cubed
¼ cup honey
2 teaspoons minced fresh dill
Salt and ground black pepper to taste

In a saucepan over medium-high heat, combine chicken stock and vinegar; reduce by half. Turn heat to low; add butter, one cube at a time. Stir in honey and dill. Remove from heat. Season with salt and pepper.

Cajun Scallops with Honey Butter Sauce

Crawfish Boil

CRAWFISH BOIL

Southerners love crawfish!

4 cups salt, divided
40–45 pounds live crawfish, divided
5 (3-ounce) bags crab boil
2 (12-ounce) cans beer
10 onions, peeled, quartered, and divided
3 pounds new potatoes, skin on, scrubbed, and
*   divided*
12 heads garlic, peeled, quartered, and divided
12 ears corn, halved and divided
12 lemons, halved

Fill ice chest with water and 2 cups salt, stir, and add crawfish. Purge for 40 minutes.

Pour 12 gallons water into 20-gallon pot. Add remaining 2 cups salt, crab boil, and beer. Boil for 15 minutes. In basket insert, place half of garlic, onions, and potatoes. Place basket in water, and boil for 5 minutes. Add half of corn and return to boil. Drain crawfish from purging water; add half to basket, and bring to rolling boil. Turn off heat, cover, and let soak for 10 minutes. Remove basket and dump contents onto newspaper-lined table. Add lemons. Repeat with remaining ingredients.
Yield: 12–16 servings

SHRIMP BOIL

2 tablespoons Old Bay Seasoning
2 pounds small red potatoes, skin on
1 pound spicy smoked link sausage, cut into
*   1½-inch pieces*
3 ears fresh corn, halved
1 large Vidalia onion, quartered
2 pounds unpeeled large shrimp

Fill large pot halfway with water and add Old Bay Seasoning. Bring to a boil. Add potatoes; return to a boil and cook for 10 minutes. Add sausage, corn, and onion; return to a boil and cook for 10 minutes. Add shrimp, and cook 3–5 minutes, or until shrimp are pink. Remove contents with a slotted spoon to platter or table lined with newspaper. Sprinkle additional Old Bay Seasoning over top, and serve with cocktail sauce, lemon, or melted butter.
Yield: 4–6 servings

BARBEQUED SHRIMP

3–4 pounds jumbo shrimp, heads on with shells
1 cup olive oil
Juice of 8 lemons
¾ cup Worcestershire sauce
¼ cup Tabasco sauce
2 tablespoons kosher salt
Cracked black pepper
2 sticks butter, cut into 1-inch pieces

Place shrimp in a 9x13-inch glass baking dish. Toss in olive oil, lemon juice, Worcestershire, and Tabasco. Sprinkle with salt and cover with pepper. Place butter pats over shrimp. Heat broiler to high, and place rack 6 inches from heat. Broil shrimp for 10–15 minutes, turning pan for even cooking. Remove, and let rest 10 minutes before serving in sauce with French bread for dipping.
Yield: 4–6 servings

SHRIMP IN PASTRY SHELLS

SHELLS:
½ cup very cold butter, cut into 8 pieces
1⅓ cups all-purpose flour
¼ cup ice water
6 large scallop shells

Preheat oven to 400 degrees. In food processor, pulse butter and flour until consistency of peas. With processor running, pour ice water in a steady stream into tube. Stop processing when dough starts to form a ball. Handling as little as possible, form dough into a flat disk about 6 inches in diameter. Cut disk into 6 wedges. Roll each wedge to fit the back side of each scallop shell. Butter shells, and press one pastry wedge over each shell, pinching off excess. Place shells on a baking sheet, and bake for 15–20 minutes, until dry and crisp. Shells can be made several days ahead or can be frozen on the shells for protection. If frozen, thaw, and heat 5–7 minutes at 350 degrees.
Yield: 6 shells

FILLING:
1½ pounds raw Gulf shrimp, peeled and deveined
½ stick plus 2 tablespoons butter, divided
White bulbs of 5 green onions, finely chopped
½ pound fresh mushrooms, sliced
1 tablespoon flour
1½ cups sour cream, room temperature
Salt to taste

Pat shrimp dry on paper towels. Sauté onions in ½ stick butter until translucent. Add shrimp, and sauté 3–5 minutes, until pink and just cooked. Remove from skillet and keep warm. Sprinkle mushrooms with flour. Add remaining 2 tablespoons butter to skillet, and sauté floured mushrooms for 2–3 minutes, stirring constantly. Reduce heat, and add shrimp mixture, sour cream, and salt. Cook mixture for several minutes, until shrimp are thoroughly heated. Do not let mixture boil. Fill pastry shells with mixture and serve immediately.
Yield: 6 servings

SHRIMP AND ANGEL HAIR PASTA

1 stick butter
1 (16-ounce) package angel hair pasta
2 cloves garlic, minced
½ cup pine nuts, ground in food processor
Salt and black pepper to taste
1 pound steamed shrimp, deveined
Parmesan cheese

In a skillet, brown butter on low heat, about 15 minutes, until it turns medium brown. While browning butter, bring pasta water to a boil; cook pasta, and drain. Add garlic to butter, and sauté. Add pine nuts, salt, and pepper to taste. Pour over drained pasta. Toss with shrimp, and sprinkle with cheese.
Yield: 4–6 servings

STUFFED CRAB

A perfect entrée for a special dinner!

1 cup mayonnaise
1 cup milk
1 pound fresh lump crabmeat, picked
2 tablespoons grated white bulbs of green onions
1 cup fresh bread crumbs, crusts removed
4 hard-cooked eggs, finely chopped
2 tablespoons melted butter
1 cup cracker crumbs

Preheat oven to 350 degrees. Whisk together mayonnaise and milk; add crabmeat, onions, bread crumbs, and eggs. Fill 6 small ramekins or crab shells. Top with combined butter and crumbs. Bake for 20 minutes or until hot and crumbs are lightly browned.
Yield: 6 servings

Shrimp in
Pastry Shells

VEGETABLES AND SIDES

FIELD PEAS

2 slices bacon
2 pounds fresh field peas, shelled and washed
4 tablespoons margarine
Salt and black pepper to taste

Bring 6 cups water and bacon to a rolling boil. Add peas; return to a boil. Reduce heat and simmer, covered, for 20 minutes or until peas are done. Turn off heat; stir in margarine and salt.
Yield: 12 servings

OVEN FRIED CORN

8 ears corn, cleaned and washed
½–¾ cup milk, divided
Salt and black pepper to taste
4 tablespoons butter

Preheat oven to 350 degrees. With knife, cut corn from cob, and rake cob into the bowl, getting juice. Add ½ cup milk, salt, and pepper to taste. Melt butter in a cast-iron skillet. Add corn mixture. Bake, uncovered, for 45 minutes, stirring often. Add additional ¼ cup milk, if it becomes too dry.
Yield: 8–10 servings

CORN CASSEROLE

1 cup biscuit mix
1 (14½-ounce) can yellow cream-style corn
2 tablespoons oil
1 egg, beaten
½ cup milk
1 (4-ounce) can chopped green chiles, drained
6 ounces Monterey Jack cheese, sliced

Preheat oven to 400 degrees. Combine biscuit mix, corn, oil, egg, and milk. Spread half of mixture in greased 8x8-inch pan. Sprinkle with chiles and cover with cheese slices. Spread remaining batter over the top. Bake for 30 minutes or until golden brown.
Yield: 6–8 servings

SWEET AND SOUR GREEN BEANS

6 slices bacon
3 (14½-ounce) cans cut Italian green beans
¾ cup slivered almonds, lightly toasted
½ cup vinegar
½ cup sugar

In a large saucepan, fry bacon until crisp. Remove bacon from pan, crumble, and set aside. To saucepan with bacon grease, add green beans and liquid, almonds, vinegar, and sugar. Simmer for 30–40 minutes. Stir in bacon.
Yield: 8–10 servings

BROILED TOMATOES

3 tablespoons butter, melted
3 tablespoons Italian bread crumbs
2 tomatoes, halved
¼ cup shredded Parmesan cheese

Preheat oven to broil. Combine butter and bread crumbs. Place on flat sides of tomatoes; sprinkle with cheese. Broil until cheese melts.
Yield: 4 servings

LIMA BEANS

2 slices ham
2 pounds fresh lima beans, shelled and washed
4 tablespoons margarine
Salt and black pepper to taste

Bring 6 cups water and ham to a rolling boil. Add beans; return to a boil. Reduce heat and simmer, covered, for 15 minutes or until beans are easily pierced with fork. Turn off heat; stir in margarine, salt, and pepper.
Yield: 12 servings

ASPARAGUS WITH LEMON ZEST AND PINE NUTS

2 tablespoons pine nuts
1½ pounds fresh asparagus, trimmed
1 tablespoon olive oil
Juice of 1 lemon
Zest of 1 lemon
½ teaspoon salt
Freshly ground black pepper

In a skillet, toast pine nuts, stirring constantly, until golden; set aside. Cut asparagus spears about 5 inches long; cut remaining stalks into tiny rounds. In a saucepan, bring water and salt to a boil, drop in asparagus, and boil for 5 minutes. Immediately remove to a bowl of ice water. Remove asparagus from water, and drizzle with olive oil and lemon juice. Sprinkle with lemon zest, salt, pepper, and pine nuts.
Yield: 6–8 servings

BROCCOLI WITH HORSERADISH SAUCE

This sauce is great on any green vegetable.

2 bunches fresh broccoli
Salt to taste

Wash and trim broccoli, and cook in boiling water for 8–10 minutes or until crisp-tender. Sprinkle with salt. Serve with Horseradish Sauce.
Yield: 8–10 servings

HORSERADISH SAUCE:
½ stick butter, melted
¾ cup mayonnaise
1½ tablespoons horseradish
¼ teaspoon salt
¼ teaspoon dry mustard
½ teaspoon ground red pepper

Combine all ingredients. (Sauce will keep in refrigerator for several months.)

Asparagus with Lemon Zest and Pine Nuts

EGGPLANT DELUXE

4 slices white bread, crumbled
2 cups milk
2 large eggplants, peeled and sliced
½ onion, chopped
2 eggs, beaten
1 cup grated Cheddar cheese
Salt and black pepper to taste

Soak bread crumbs in the milk; set aside. Soak eggplant slices in salted water 30 minutes; drain. In a saucepan with water to cover, boil eggplants and onion until tender. Remove from heat, and drain. Add eggs, cheese, bread crumbs, salt, and pepper. Pour into greased casserole. Preheat oven to 350 degrees. Bake for 30 minutes.
Yield: 8–10 servings

VEGGIE STRATA

½ stick butter, melted
6 slices white bread
2 heads broccoli flowerets, chopped
½ each: red and yellow bell pepper, chopped
½ red onion, chopped
2 tomatoes, chopped
3 cups shredded sharp Cheddar cheese
6 large eggs, slightly beaten
3¼ cups half-and-half
¼ teaspoon dry mustard
Salt and black pepper to taste
Paprika for sprinkling

Pour butter in a 9x13-inch casserole. Layer bread and vegetables, and cover with cheese. Combine eggs, half-and-half, dry mustard, salt, and pepper. Pour over cheese. Sprinkle with paprika. Chill overnight. Preheat oven to 325 degrees. Bring casserole to room temperature for 30 minutes. Bake for 30 minutes. Raise temperature to 350 degrees, and bake an additional 25–30 minutes, until set and browned.
Yield: 8–10 servings

SIMPLY GREAT GREEN BEANS

This is everyone's favorite easy vegetable.

6 (14½-ounce) cans whole green beans
½ stick butter
½ cup packed brown sugar
½ cup Hormel real crumbled bacon

Preheat oven to 325 degrees. Drain green beans, and pour into greased 9x13-inch baking dish. Set aside. Melt butter, and stir in brown sugar. Pour butter and sugar mixture over green beans. Sprinkle with crumbled bacon. Cover with foil, and bake for 30 minutes.
Yield: 12–16 servings

GREEN BEANS WITH CREAM SAUCE

1¼ cups mayonnaise
1 onion, finely grated, and juice
1 teaspoon dry mustard
1 cup grated sharp Cheddar cheese
1 teaspoon Worcestershire sauce
1 teaspoon salt
2 (14½-ounce) cans green beans, drained
1 (8-ounce) can sliced water chestnuts, drained and chopped

Preheat oven to 350 degrees. Combine mayonnaise, onion and juice, dry mustard, cheese, Worcestershire, and salt. In a 9x13-inch baking dish, layer beans, water chestnuts, and mayonnaise mixture. Bake for 35 minutes.
Yield: 6 servings

Simply Great
Green Beans

ROASTED VEGETABLES

1 red bell pepper, sliced
1 yellow bell pepper, sliced
1 large zucchini, sliced
1 large yellow squash, sliced
1 cup baby carrots
1 onion, sliced
1 bunch asparagus, trimmed and cut
3 tablespoons olive oil
Zest and juice of 1 lemon
1 teaspoon lemon pepper

Preheat oven to 375 degrees. Toss vegetables with olive oil, lemon juice and zest, and seasoning. Place on a foil-lined rimmed baking sheet. Bake uncovered for 20–30 minutes.
Yield: 12–16 servings

SPINACH AND ARTICHOKE CASSEROLE

2 (10-ounce) packages frozen chopped spinach, thawed
½ onion, chopped
4 tablespoons butter
1 (8-ounce) carton sour cream
½ cup grated Parmesan cheese
1 (14-ounce) can artichoke hearts, drained and chopped
1 teaspoon seasoned salt
½ stick butter, melted
1 stack saltine crackers, crushed

Steam spinach slightly, drain, and set aside. Sauté onion in butter. Preheat oven to 350 degrees. Combine spinach, onion, sour cream, cheese, artichoke hearts, and salt. Pour into a greased 2-quart baking dish. Combine butter and crackers, and sprinkle on top. Bake for 30 minutes.
Yield: 8–10 servings

Roasted Vegetables

POTATO CASSEROLE WITH WHIPPED CREAM

½ small onion, grated
1 stick plus 2 tablespoons butter, melted, divided
5 pounds white potatoes, peeled and boiled
1 (8-ounce) package cream cheese, softened
1 (8-ounce) carton sour cream
¼ cup chopped chives
Salt and ground black pepper to taste
½ pint heavy cream, whipped
1 cup shredded Cheddar cheese
½ cup real bacon bits

Preheat oven to 350 degrees. Sauté onion in 2 tablespoons butter, and set aside. Drain potatoes; mash until creamy. Add cream cheese, remaining 1 stick melted butter, sour cream, sautéed onions, chives, salt, and pepper. Spread into a greased 9x13-inch baking dish. Spread with whipped cream and sprinkle with cheese and bacon. Bake 20 minutes. Place under broiler a few minutes to lightly brown.
Yield: 10–12 servings

PARMESAN BAKED POTATOES

5 pounds potatoes, sliced
Salt and black pepper to taste
2 (8-ounce) cartons whipped cream
2 tablespoons Dijon mustard
2 tablespoons butter
½ cup grated Parmesan cheese

Preheat oven to 350 degrees. In a greased 9x13-inch baking dish, layer potatoes. Sprinkle with salt and pepper; set aside. In a saucepan, combine cream, mustard, and butter. Heat to boiling, and pour over potatoes. Cover with foil, and bake for 1 hour. Uncover, and sprinkle with cheese. Bake for an additional 10 minutes.
Yield: 6–8 servings

NEW POTATOES IN CREAM SAUCE

This is perfect served with any meat.

4 pounds new red potatoes
1 teaspoon salt
2 tablespoons butter
2 tablespoons all-purpose flour
1 cup milk
Salt and black pepper to taste

Wash and scrub potatoes with a brush. If potatoes are over 2 inches in diameter, cut in half. Place in a saucepan, and cover with water. Add 1 teaspoon salt. Boil 15–20 minutes, until tender; drain. In a saucepan, melt butter and stir in flour; add milk. Mix well. Pour flour mixture over potatoes; add salt and pepper. Simmer about 10 minutes until cream sauce is thickened. If too thick, add more milk.
Yield: 12 servings

GLAZED CARROTS

1 pound fresh baby carrots
½ cup cornstarch
2 tablespoons cold water
½ cup lemon juice
2 tablespoons butter
1 teaspoon vanilla

In a saucepan over medium heat, cook carrots 15 minutes in water to cover; set aside. In a bowl, combine cornstarch and 2 tablespoons cold water. Add to carrots; cook for an additional 10–15 minutes until tender. Stir in lemon juice, butter, and vanilla.
Yield: 6–8 servings

Caramelized Onion Gratin Pots

CARAMELIZED ONION GRATIN POTS

1½ tablespoons butter
3 Vidalia onions, thinly sliced
3 garlic cloves, minced
2 tablespoons sugar
1 cup heavy cream
4 large eggs
1 cup ricotta cheese
½ cup grated Swiss cheese
Salt and black pepper to taste
For garnish: fresh chives

In large skillet, melt butter over medium heat. Add onions and garlic; cook until soft, about 5 minutes. Add sugar and cook until onions are caramelized, about 10 minutes; set aside. Whisk cream and eggs to blend. Whisk in cheeses, salt, and pepper. Blend in onions. Generously butter 8 (4-ounce) ramekins. Preheat oven to 350 degrees. Transfer mixture to prepared dishes. Bake about 25 minutes or until knife inserted in center comes out clean. Garnish with chives.
Yield: 8 servings

MUSHROOM RIGATONI

1 tablespoon olive oil
1 cup chopped shallots (about 6)
½ pound mushrooms, stemmed and sliced
⅓ cup white wine
1½ cups tomato sauce
¼ cup chopped flat leaf parsley
Salt and black pepper to taste
⅓ cup heavy cream
¾ pound rigatoni
Parmesan cheese, grated, to taste

In a saucepan, heat oil over medium heat. Add shallots and mushrooms. Cook 3–4 minutes, or until vegetables are soft. Add wine and cook for 2–3 minutes or until evaporated. Add tomato sauce, parsley, salt, and pepper. Bring to a simmer and cook 4–5 minutes. Stir in cream. Simmer uncovered for 2 minutes. Cook pasta 7–9 minutes; drain and mix with sauce. Sprinkle Parmesan on top.
Yield: 6–8 servings

MACARONI AND CHEESE

This is a comfort dish for sure!

1 (16-ounce) box elbow macaroni
1½ (10-ounce) packages Cracker Barrel extra sharp
    Cheddar cheese, grated, divided
1 stick butter, melted
6 eggs, beaten
1 teaspoon salt
2 cups half-and-half

Cook macaroni until tender. Drain. Preheat oven to 300 degrees. Add all but ¼ cup grated cheese with melted butter to macaroni. Add beaten eggs and salt. Add half-and-half. Sprinkle with remaining ¼ cup cheese. Bake for 30 minutes.
Yield: 6–8 servings

ORZO WITH VEGETABLES

1 (16-ounce) package orzo
1 eggplant, chopped
1 each: red, orange, and yellow bell pepper,
    chopped
1 purple onion, chopped
1 cup grape tomatoes, halved
¼ cup olive oil, divided
4 ounces feta cheese
Juice of 1 lemon

Cook orzo according to package directions; set aside. Preheat oven to 350 degrees. Place vegetable in foil-lined 9x13-inch baking dish; drizzle with ⅛ cup olive oil, and bake for 10 minutes. Combine orzo, roasted veggies, and feta in a large bowl. Drizzle with remaining olive oil and lemon juice. Serve at room temperature.
Yield: 12 servings

HEIRLOOM TOMATO PIE

1 (9-inch) pie crust
5 large heirloom tomatoes, sliced
Salt and Ac'cent to taste
10 fresh basil leaves, chopped
1 small bunch chives, chopped
1 cup mayonnaise
1 cup shredded sharp Cheddar cheese
For garnish: sliced tomatoes, fresh basil, and
    shredded cheese

Preheat oven to 400 degrees. Bake pie crust according to package directions until almost done; set aside to cool. Drain tomatoes in colander; sprinkle with salt and Ac'cent. Layer tomatoes in pie crust. Sprinkle with fresh herbs. Repeat layers. Combine mayonnaise and cheese and spread on top of pie. (Pimiento cheese is a good alternate topping.) Wrap edges of pie with foil. Bake for 8–10 minutes until bubbly and brown on top. Serve at room temperature garnished with tomatoes, basil leaves, and cheese.
Yield: 6 servings

MARINATED TOMATOES

⅔ cup oil
1 cup sugar
¼ cup apple cider vinegar
½ small onion, grated
4 (14½-ounce) cans tomato wedges, well drained

Combine oil, sugar, vinegar, and onion. Pour over tomatoes. Chill overnight. When ready to serve, drain again.
Yield: 12 servings

BAKED SWEET POTATO FRIES

6 sweet potatoes, cut into strips
2 tablespoons oil
1 teaspoon pumpkin pie spice
Salt and black pepper to taste

Preheat oven to 400 degrees. Toss fries in oil and spices. Spread in a single layer on baking sheet lined with foil. Bake 30 minutes, turning once. Serve warm with Curry Dip.
Yield: 6–8 servings

CURRY DIP:

1 cup mayonnaise
½ teaspoon dry mustard
1½ teaspoons curry powder
½ teaspoon paprika
¼ teaspoon red pepper

Combine ingredients. Serve at room temperature.

SWEET POTATO SOUFFLÉ

6 cups cooked and mashed sweet potatoes
1 cup sugar
2 eggs, well beaten
½ teaspoon salt
1 teaspoon vanilla
1 stick margarine, softened, divided
½ cup milk
1 cup light brown sugar
⅓ cup all-purpose flour
1 cup chopped pecans
1 cup shredded coconut

Preheat oven to 350 degrees. Combine potatoes, sugar, eggs, salt, vanilla, ½ stick margarine, and milk, and pour into a greased baking dish. Combine remaining ½ stick margarine, brown sugar, flour, pecans, and coconut, and sprinkle on top. Bake for 35 minutes.
Yield: 10–12 servings

YELLOW SQUASH CASSEROLE

This is my favorite squash casserole.

2 cups cooked cubed yellow squash
1 teaspoon sugar
½ cup mayonnaise
½ cup chopped onion
¼ cup each: finely chopped green and red bell pepper
1 tablespoon butter
1 egg, slightly beaten
½ cup shredded Swiss cheese
½ stick margarine, melted
½ cup saltine cracker crumbs

Preheat oven to 350 degrees. Blend squash with sugar and mayonnaise. Sauté onion and bell peppers in butter until tender. Stir egg and cheese into onion and bell peppers. Mix onion mixture with squash mixture, and spread into a greased 9x9-inch casserole dish. Combine margarine and cracker crumbs. Spread evenly over top of casserole. Bake 30 minutes.
Yield: 6–8 servings

COMPANY RICE

1½ cups long-grain rice
1 (14½-ounce) can chicken broth
1 clove garlic, minced
1 medium onion, sliced in half moons
1 cup coarsely chopped pecans
1 stick margarine
½ cup chopped parsley
1 cup halved grapes
Salt to taste

Cook rice according to package directions, using chicken broth instead of water, and set aside. In a large frying pan, sauté garlic, onion, and pecans in margarine until tender. Add rice, parsley, grapes, and salt; continue to cook on low until heated.
Yield: 6–8 servings

CORNBREAD DRESSING

1 cup chopped onion

½ stick butter

1 cup each: chopped bell pepper and celery

2 (14½-ounce) cans chicken broth, divided

2 tablespoons Worcestershire sauce

Tabasco sauce, salt, and black pepper to taste

1 (9-ounce) skillet cornbread, crumbled

6 slices white bread, torn into small pieces

1 (4-ounce) can sliced mushrooms, drained

1 (8-ounce) can water chestnuts, drained, chopped

4 eggs, lightly beaten

Preheat oven to 400 degrees. Sauté onion in butter; set aside. Simmer bell pepper and celery in 1½ cups chicken broth. Add Worcestershire, Tabasco, salt, and pepper; set aside. Combine breads; add onions and chicken broth mixture. Stir in mushrooms, water chestnuts, and eggs. Moisten with remaining chicken broth. Pour into greased 9x13-inch baking dish. Bake 1 hour. Yield: 12–16 servings

APPLE-CRANBERRY BAKE

My family requests this at Thanksgiving and Christmas. It is also great as a warm dessert served with ice cream.

3 Granny Smith apples, unpeeled and chopped

2 cups fresh cranberries

1 tablespoon lemon juice

¾ cup sugar

1 stick butter, melted

1 cup uncooked oatmeal

½ cup all-purpose flour

½ cup packed light brown sugar

1 cup chopped pecans

Preheat oven to 350 degrees. Combine apples, cranberries, lemon juice, and sugar. Place in a greased 9x11-inch baking dish. Combine butter, oatmeal, flour, brown sugar, and pecans. Crumble over fruit. Bake 1 hour.
Yield: 8–10 servings

Yellow Squash Casserole , Apple-Cranberry Bake , Sweet Potato Soufflé, and Cornbread Dressing

Morning Glory Muffins
and Orange Muffins

BREADS AND MUFFINS

BUTTERMILK BISCUITS

1 cup self-rising flour (or a little more if
   necessary)
1½ cups buttermilk
⅓ cup vegetable shortening

Preheat oven to 400 degrees. Combine flour,
buttermilk, and shortening. Dough will be
sticky. Knead dough, and pat out biscuits to
desired size. Place in a greased hot iron skillet.
Coat top of biscuits with shortening. Bake for
20–25 minutes.
Yield: 8–10 biscuits

CHEDDAR BACON BISCUITS

4 slices bacon
2 cups self-rising flour
2 teaspoons baking powder
1 tablespoon chopped fresh chives
6 tablespoons cold unsalted butter, cut into small
   pieces, plus melted butter for brushing
1 cup grated Cheddar cheese
1 cup buttermilk

Preheat oven to 425 degrees. Cook bacon until
crisp, drain, reserving 2 tablespoons drippings,
and crumble. In medium bowl, whisk together
flour, baking powder, bacon bits, and chives. Using a pastry blender, cut butter into flour. Stir in
the cheese. Add buttermilk and reserved bacon
drippings, and gently mix until just moistened.
Turn dough onto a lightly floured surface, and
knead 3 or 4 times, until dough comes together.
Roll out to ½ inch thick, then cut out biscuits
using a 2-inch cutter dipped in flour. Place on an
ungreased baking sheet. Brush tops with melted
butter. Bake 12–15 minutes.
Yield: 18–20 biscuits

SOUR CREAM BISCUITS

1 stick butter, melted
1 tablespoon buttermilk
1 (8-ounce) container sour cream
2 cups biscuit mix

Preheat oven to 425 degrees. Grease miniature
muffin tins. Combine ingredients, and blend
thoroughly with a fork. Drop one tablespoon
batter into each greased miniature muffin cup,
and bake for 12 minutes.
Yield: 30–36 mini biscuits

SWEET POTATO BISCUITS

2 cups sweet potatoes
3 sticks butter, melted and divided
1 teaspoon salt
1½ teaspoons ground cinnamon
1 teaspoon ground ginger
½ teaspoon ground allspice
1 cup packed light brown sugar
5 cups all-purpose flour
2 tablespoons baking powder
1 cup heavy cream
Confectioners' sugar

Preheat oven to 425 degrees. Roast sweet
potatoes until very tender, then cool, peel,
and mash. Add 2 sticks butter, salt, cinnamon,
ginger, and allspice. Add brown sugar. Combine
flour and baking powder. Add flour mixture to
potato mixture. Add cream to make soft dough.
Roll out dough to 1½ inches thick. Cut out with
2-inch round cookie cutter dipped in flour. Place
biscuits 1 inch apart on ungreased cookie sheet.
Bake 10 minutes. If additional baking time is
needed, turn temperature down to 375 degrees
and bake until golden brown. Brush with melted
butter and sprinkle with confectioners' sugar.
Yield: 40–48 small biscuits

EASY ROLLS

1 cup warm water
1 tablespoon RapidRise yeast
1 tablespoon sugar
3 cups bread flour
1 teaspoon salt
2 tablespoons olive oil

Heat water in microwave for 30 seconds. Mix in yeast and sugar until foamy; set aside. Place flour and salt in food processor. Pour in olive oil, and pulse 30 seconds. Add yeast mixture, and process 20–30 seconds. Place dough in greased bowl. Cover with a towel, and let rise 1 hour. Preheat oven to 400 degrees. For cloverleaf rolls, roll dough into small balls. Place 3 small balls into each section of greased muffin tin. Let rise 15 minutes. Bake 10–12 minutes.
Yield: 2 dozen rolls

YEAST ROLLS

These are my favorite rolls. They turn out perfect every time.

1 (¼-ounce) package RapidRise yeast
¼ cup warm water
½ stick butter
¼ cup sugar
4 cups all-purpose flour
1 teaspoon salt
1 cup scalded milk
1 egg, beaten

Dissolve yeast in warm water; set aside. Cream butter, adding sugar slowly. Sift flour and salt together; set aside. Mix milk, egg, and yeast mixture together and stir into the butter mixture. Slowly stir flour mixture into yeast mixture to form soft dough. Chill dough 12 hours. Roll out dough and cut into small circles. Let rise in a warm place for 2 hours, and bake at 425 degrees for 10–13 minutes.
Yield: 2–3 dozen rolls

Easy Rolls

CORNBREAD

2 cups self-rising cornmeal
½ cup all-purpose flour
1 egg
¾ cup buttermilk
¼ cup water
2 teaspoons vegetable shortening, melted and
    divided

Preheat oven to 400 degrees. Mix together
cornmeal, flour, egg, buttermilk, water, and 1
teaspoon melted shortening. Heat remaining
teaspoon of shortening in a 10-inch iron skillet
or muffin tin in oven. Sprinkle skillet or muffin
tin with a small amount of cornmeal. Pour in
batter. Bake for 20 minutes.
Yield: 8 servings or 12 muffins

SPICY CORNBREAD

½ cup oil, divided
1½ cups cornmeal, divided
½ teaspoon salt
½ cup chopped onion
1 cup grated Cheddar cheese
3 eggs
3 jalapeño peppers, chopped
1 (2-ounce) jar diced pimientos, drained
1 (14¾-ounce) can cream-style corn
½ cup milk

Preheat oven to 350 degrees. Grease a well-
seasoned 10-inch black iron skillet with 2
tablespoons oil, then heat in oven until very
hot; remove, and sprinkle skillet bottom with
1 tablespoon cornmeal. Combine remaining
ingredients, and pour into skillet. Bake 45–50
minutes.
Yield: 8 servings

POPOVERS

These are great with fillings and make a pretty
presentation for entrées or desserts.

1 cup all-purpose flour
½ teaspoon salt
1 cup milk
2 eggs

Preheat oven to 425 degrees. In mixer or blender, combine all ingredients and until smooth.
Pour into well-greased muffin cups or popover
tins to about ¾ full. Bake for about 35 minutes.
Gently remove popover from tin. Puncture with
tip of sharp knife then slice off top. Serve with
butter and jam or add a filling. For hot fillings,
popovers can be filled and returned to oven for
10 minutes at 300 degrees on a baking sheet.
Yield: 6 large or 12 small popovers

FILLINGS FOR POPOVERS:
Chicken or shrimp in a cream sauce
Cooked broccoli sprinkled with Cheddar cheese
    or sauce
Scrambled eggs sprinkled with cheese, bacon
    bits, chopped ham, peppers, and onions
Hot chili topped with shredded cheese and green
    onions
Chicken salad, ham salad, or tuna salad
Lemon curd with fresh berries
Strawberries and whipped cream
Custard with chocolate sauce

Popovers

SOURDOUGH BREAD

STARTER:

1 package dry yeast
1 cup very warm water, divided
¾ cup sugar
3 tablespoons instant potato flakes

Dissolve yeast in ½ cup warm water. Combine with remaining water, sugar, and potato flakes; let stand at room temperature for 8–12 hours, uncovered. Refrigerate in covered plastic or glass container. After 3 days, feed Starter according to recipe below.

TO FEED STARTER:

1 cup very warm water
¾ cup sugar
3 tablespoons instant potato flakes

Add above ingredients; leave uncovered at room temperature for 8–12 hours before placing back in refrigerator. Starter must be fed at least every 7 days, but can be fed as often as every 3 days. If container is full and you are not planning to use Starter to make bread, pour 1 cup of Starter off to make room to feed.

BREAD:

1 cup Starter
1½ cups very warm water
2 teaspoons salt
¼ cup sugar
½ cup oil
6 cups all-purpose flour or bread flour

Draw off 1 cup Starter, and mix with warm water, salt, sugar, and oil. Add flour, 1 cup at a time, and mix. Pour dough out on a floured board; knead. Add flour as needed to make into a nonsticky dough ball. Place dough in greased bowl; cover with towel for 8–12 hours or until doubled in size. Remove dough, and place on floured board. Knead gently 5–6 times. Divide into 3 parts; place in greased bread pans. Cover with plastic wrap; allow to rise at room temperature for 8–12 hours. Bake at 325 degrees for about 30 minutes or until light golden brown.
Yield: 3 loaves

BANANA BREAD

2¼ cups all-purpose flour
1 teaspoon baking powder
1 teaspoon baking soda
½ teaspoon salt
½ teaspoon cinnamon
½ teaspoon vanilla
6 large, ripe bananas, mashed
½ cup sugar
2 eggs, beaten
¼ cup vegetable oil
1 cup chopped walnuts
1 cup flaked coconut

Preheat oven to 350 degrees. Combine flour, baking powder, baking soda, salt, and cinnamon. Add vanilla, bananas, sugar, eggs, and oil. Mix just until moistened. Stir in walnuts and coconut. Bake in 2 greased loaf pans for 20–30 minutes.
Yield: 2 loaves

DATE NUT BREAD

This bread is perfect for gifts. It is such a treat.

2 eggs, beaten
1 cup sugar
1 cup all-purpose flour
1 teaspoon baking powder
½ teaspoon salt
¼ cup milk
1 teaspoon vanilla
1 (8-ounce) package dates, chopped
1 pound pecan halves

Preheat oven to 325 degrees. Mix well by hand, eggs, sugar, flour, baking powder, and salt. Add milk and vanilla. Stir in dates and pecans. Bake in 2 greased loaf pans for 1 hour. Cool and slice with electric knife. Freezes well.
Yield: 2 loaves

MORNING GLORY MUFFINS

People from all around visit Broad Street Baking Company in Jackson, Mississippi, for these delicious muffins.

1¼ cups sugar

2¼ cups all-purpose flour

1 tablespoon cinnamon

2 teaspoons baking soda

½ teaspoon salt

½ cup sweetened shredded coconut

½ cup dark raisins

1 Red Delicious apple, shredded

1 (8-ounce) can crushed pineapple, drained

2 cups grated carrots

½ cup chopped pecans

3 eggs

1 cup canola oil

1 teaspoon vanilla

Preheat oven to 375 degrees. Sift together sugar, flour, cinnamon, baking soda, and salt into a large mixing bowl. Stir in coconut, raisins, apple, pineapple, carrots, and pecans. In another bowl, whisk eggs, oil, and vanilla. Pour into dry ingredients, and mix well. Spoon batter into greased muffin tins to slightly above the rim. Bake for 35 minutes or until a toothpick comes out clean. Let cool for at least 10 minutes; turn out on a wire rack.
Yield: 12 muffins

ORANGE MUFFINS

2 sticks butter, softened

1 cup sugar

2 eggs

1 teaspoon baking soda

1 cup buttermilk

2 cups all-purpose flour

½ cup raisins

Zest and juice of 2 oranges

1 cup brown sugar

Preheat oven to 375 degrees. Cream butter and sugar; beat in eggs, and set aside. Dissolve soda in buttermilk, and set aside. Mix flour with raisins and orange zest. Beat flour and buttermilk, alternately, into creamed mixture. Bake in greased muffin tins for 20 minutes. Mix brown sugar and orange juice. Dip warm muffins in juice mixture, and drain on rack.
Yield: 12 muffins

PRALINE MUFFINS

1¼ cups coarsely chopped pecans

1 cup packed light brown sugar

½ cup all-purpose flour

2 eggs, beaten

½ teaspoon vanilla

1 stick butter, melted

Preheat oven to 325 degrees. Combine pecans, brown sugar, and flour. Add eggs, vanilla, and butter. Stir well. Spoon into greased mini muffin pans, filling half full. Bake for 16–20 minutes.
Yield: 24 muffins

BLUEBERRY MUFFINS

2 cups biscuit mix
¾ cup sugar
1 cup sour cream
1 egg
1 teaspoon vanilla
1 (6-ounce) container fresh blueberries

Preheat oven to 450 degrees. Combine biscuit mix and sugar; make a well in the center. Add sour cream, egg, and vanilla; mix with a fork. Fold in berries. Spoon into greased muffin tins. Sprinkle Topping on muffins. Bake 15–20 minutes.
Yield: 8 muffins

TOPPING:

Zest and juice of 1 lemon
2½ tablespoons sugar
1 teaspoon cinnamon

Combine ingredients.

PEACH MUFFINS

1 stick butter, softened
¾ cup sugar
1 egg
½ cup sour cream
1 teaspoon vanilla
¼ teaspoon almond extract
1½ cups all-purpose flour
1½ teaspoons baking powder
1 cup chopped fresh or frozen peaches
1 cup chopped pecans

Preheat oven to 400 degrees. With mixer, cream butter and sugar. Beat in egg. Add sour cream and flavorings. Sift together flour and baking powder; stir in by hand. Stir in peaches and nuts. Drop into greased miniature muffin tins. Bake for 15 minutes or until lightly browned.
Yield: 48 muffins

Chocolate Rose Cake, White Chocolate Magnolia Cake, and Lemon Daffodil Cake

CAKES

CHOCOLATE ROSE CAKE

1 (18¼-ounce) box butter cake mix
1 (3-ounce) box instant chocolate pudding mix
2 tablespoons cocoa
1 stick butter, softened
1⅓ cups water
3 eggs, room temperature

Preheat oven to 350 degrees. With mixer, combine cake mix, pudding mix, and cocoa in a large mixing bowl. Beat in butter, water, and eggs on low speed until well blended. Beat on medium speed for 2 minutes. Pour batter into 3 greased and floured 9-inch round pans, smoothing batter. Bake for 20–22 minutes. Cool in pans for 5 minutes. Turn out, and cool on a wire rack until completely cool before frosting.
Yield: 12–16 servings

CHOCOLATE BUTTERCREAM FROSTING:

1 (12-ounce) package semisweet chocolate chips
1½ sticks butter
½ cup half-and-half
6 cups confectioners' sugar, sifted
1 teaspoon vanilla

In a saucepan over medium heat, combine chips, butter, and half-and-half until chips are melted. Remove from heat to mixing bowl. With mixer, beat in sugar and vanilla, mixing well. Beat until light and fluffy. Spread between layers and frost sides and top of cake.

LEMON DAFFODIL CAKE

1 (18¼-ounce) box lemon cake mix
1 cup lemon yogurt
⅓ cup oil
1¼ cups water
3 eggs, room temperature

Preheat oven to 350 degrees. With mixer on low speed, blend cake mix, yogurt, oil, water, and eggs until well blended. Beat on medium speed for 2 minutes. Pour batter into 3 greased and floured 9-inch round pans, smoothing batter. Bake for 18–20 minutes. Cool in pans for 5 minutes. Turn out, and cool on a wire rack until completely cool before frosting.
Yield: 12–16 servings

LEMON BUTTERCREAM FROSTING:

1½ sticks butter, softened
6 cups confectioners' sugar, sifted
¼ cup fresh lemon juice
Few drops yellow food coloring

With mixer on low speed, beat butter until fluffy. Add sugar and lemon juice; blend on low speed until sugar is well incorporated. Add food coloring and increase speed to medium; beat until frosting is light and fluffy. Spread between layers and frost sides and top of cake.

WHITE CHOCOLATE MAGNOLIA CAKE

This cake is so special and beautiful.

1 (18¼-ounce) box white cake mix
1 (3¼-ounce) box white chocolate instant pudding
  mix
1⅓ cups water
⅓ cup oil
⅔ cup egg whites, room temperature
2 ounces Baker's white chocolate, melted

Preheat oven to 350 degrees. With mixer, blend
cake mix and pudding mix; add water, oil, and
egg whites. Beat at low speed until well blended. Add melted chocolate to mixture, and beat
at medium speed for 2 minutes. Pour batter into
2 greased and floured 9-inch round pans. Bake
for 25–30 minutes. Cool in pans for 5 minutes.
Turn out, and cool on a wire rack until completely cool before frosting. Split cooled layers
horizontally, and frost.
Yield: 12–16 servings

WHITE CHOCOLATE FROSTING:

1 stick butter, softened
4 cups confectioners' sugar, divided
6 tablespoons heavy cream, divided
4 squares Baker's white chocolate, melted

With mixer on low speed, beat butter, 2 cups
sugar, and 2 tablespoons cream until blended.
Add remaining sugar and cream, mixing on low
speed until well blended. Add melted chocolate
and beat on medium speed until smooth. Spread
between layers and frost sides and top of cake.

Strawberry Meringue Cake

STRAWBERRY MERINGUE CAKE

This is like a light strawberry shortcake.

1 (18¼-ounce) box yellow cake mix
2 egg whites
1 teaspoon almond extract, divided
1 teaspoon vanilla
½ cup sugar

Preheat oven to 350 degrees. Prepare cake mix according to directions on package, adding ½ teaspoon almond extract. Pour into 2 greased and floured 8-inch round cake pans; set aside. With mixer, beat egg whites, vanilla, and remaining ½ teaspoon almond extract until soft peaks form. Gradually add sugar. Beat until stiff peaks form. Drop egg white mixture onto unbaked batter in pans; carefully spread to cover. Bake for 25–30 minutes. Cool in pans for 10 minutes. Carefully remove from pans. Place cake layers meringue-side up onto wire racks to cool thoroughly. About 1–2 hours before serving, prepare Filling.
Yield: 12–16 servings

FILLING:

1 cup heavy cream
2 tablespoons confectioners' sugar
1 teaspoon vanilla
1 cup sliced fresh strawberries
For garnish: fresh whole strawberries

Combine cream, confectioners' sugar, and vanilla. Beat until soft peaks form. Fold in strawberries. Place one cake layer, meringue side up, on cake plate. Spread Filling over top. Place second layer, meringue side up, on Filling. Chill for at least 1 hour, but no more than 2 hours.

MANDARIN ORANGE CAKE

1 (18¼-ounce) box orange cake mix
1 (3-ounce) box orange gelatin
1 (11-ounce) can Mandarin oranges, drained and puréed
4 large eggs
½ cup canola oil
¼ cup water
½ teaspoon orange extract
½ (13.2-ounce) jar chilled orange marmalade

Preheat oven to 350 degrees. Lightly grease and flour 3 (8-inch) or 2 (9-inch) round cake pans; set aside. With mixer, combine cake mix and gelatin. Add oranges, eggs, oil, water, and extract, and beat 2 minutes. Pour batter into prepared pans, and bake 20 minutes or until toothpick comes out clean. Cool in pans for 10 minutes; turn out on racks, and cool 20 minutes. Freeze layers. Remove from freezer, spread marmalade between layers, and ice with Orange Frosting.
Yield: 12–16 servings

ORANGE FROSTING:

½ stick unsalted butter, softened
1 (8-ounce) package cream cheese, softened
4 ounces Mandarin oranges, drained and puréed
½ teaspoon orange extract
6–7 cups confectioners' sugar
For garnish: fresh orange peel curls and sugared flowers

With mixer, beat butter and cream cheese until creamy. Add oranges and extract. Beat in confectioners' sugar, 1 cup at a time. Beat until smooth. If frosting is too stiff, add milk.

For sugared flowers, dip pesticide-free petals in 1 egg white beaten and 1 teaspoon water. Sprinkle with sugar and dry on wire racks overnight.

ALMOND TORTE

1¼ sticks plus 1 tablespoon butter, softened,
    divided
¼ cup sliced almonds
1 (7-ounce) box almond paste, grated
1⅓ cups sugar
6 eggs, room temperature
1 teaspoon vanilla
1 cup all-purpose flour
1 teaspoon baking powder
¼ teaspoon salt
For garnish: sliced almonds

Preheat oven to 325 degrees, and position rack
in middle of oven. Line a 9-inch springform
pan with foil; then grease with 1 tablespoon
butter, and sprinkle with ¼ cup sliced almonds.

With mixer, combine almond paste and sugar to
achieve small crumbs. Add remaining 1¼ sticks
butter, and beat until light and creamy. Add
eggs, one at a time, beating after each addition.
Beat for 3 minutes, until very light and fluffy.
Add vanilla and beat until combined. Whisk
together flour, baking powder, and salt. Add to
almond paste mixture, and beat until just incorporated. Spoon batter into prepared springform
pan. Bake for 55–60 minutes, or until toothpick
inserted into center comes out clean. Cool pan
on wire rack for 15 minutes, then remove sides.
Garnish with almonds.
Yield: 10–12 servings

KAHLÚA BUNDT CAKE

1 (18¼-ounce) box chocolate fudge cake mix
¾ cup Kahlúa
2 cups sour cream
½ cup oil
2 eggs
1 (12-ounce) bag semisweet chocolate chips

Preheat oven to 350 degrees. With mixer, cream cake mix, Kahlúa, sour cream, oil, and eggs. Stir in chocolate chips. Pour into greased Bundt pan and bake 50–55 minutes. Cool in pan for 10 minutes before turning onto wire rack.
Yield: 12–16 servings

GERMAN CHOCOLATE BUNDT CAKE

This cake is so creamy, and yes, you do put all but ¼ cup of the canned frosting into the cake batter.

1 (18¼-ounce) box German chocolate cake mix
1 (12-ounce) can coconut pecan frosting (reserve ¼ cup for a glaze)
4 eggs
¾ cup oil
½ cup water
1 cup chopped pecans
Confectioners' sugar (optional)

Preheat oven to 325 degrees. Mix all ingredients together by hand, and pour batter into a well-greased and floured Bundt pan. Bake for 45–50 minutes. Cool in pan for 5 minutes on a wire rack before turning out. Spread reserved ¼ cup frosting on cake for a glaze, or sprinkle with confectioners' sugar, if desired.
Yield: 12–16 servings

WHITE CHOCOLATE POUND CAKE

1 (18¼-ounce) box yellow cake mix
1 (3¼-ounce) box white chocolate instant pudding mix
1 cup sour cream
½ cup oil
½ cup water
4 eggs
1 (12-ounce) bag white chocolate chips
4 ounces vanilla almond bark, melted

Preheat oven to 350 degrees. With mixer, combine cake mix, pudding mix, sour cream, oil, water, and eggs. Batter will be thick. Fold in chocolate chips, and pour batter into a greased and floured Bundt pan. Bake 45–50 minutes. Turn off oven and leave in oven for 1 hour. Turn onto cake plate, and drizzle with melted almond bark.
Yield: 16–20 servings

CHOCOLATE CHIP CHOCOLATE CAKE

1 (18¼-ounce) box Devil's food cake mix
1 (3¼-ounce) box chocolate instant pudding mix
1¾ cups milk
2 eggs
1 (12-ounce) bag semisweet chocolate chips

Preheat oven to 350 degrees. With mixer, combine cake mix, pudding mix, milk, and eggs. Stir in chocolate chips. Bake in a greased and sugared Bundt or tube pan for 50–60 minutes. Cool for 10 minutes before removing from pan.
Yield: 12–16 servings

FIG PRESERVE CAKE

1 (18¼-ounce) box spice cake mix
3 eggs
½ teaspoon cinnamon
1 (11½-ounce) jar fig preserves
¼ cup oil

Preheat oven to 350 degrees. Mix all ingredients together with mixer. Divide batter evenly among 3 (8-inch) greased and floured cake pans, and bake for 30 minutes or until a toothpick comes out clean. Drizzle with Caramel Frosting.
Yield: 12–16 servings

CARAMEL FROSTING:
1 stick butter, melted
1 cup firmly packed brown sugar
½ cup heavy cream

Combine butter, brown sugar, and cream. In microwave, heat for 13 minutes on LOW. Stir, and pour over warm cake.

PLANTATION CAKE

This cake is so moist.

1 (18¼-ounce) box butter cake mix
1 cup sugar
4 eggs
1 cup sour cream
¾ cup oil
1 (7-ounce) can sweetened flaked coconut
1½ cups chopped pecans, toasted

Preheat oven to 325 degrees. With mixer, combine cake mix, sugar, eggs, sour cream, and oil. Stir in coconut and pecans. Pour into greased and floured tube or Bundt pan. Bake for 1 hour and 20 minutes. Cool in pan for 10 minutes before turning out.
Yield: 12–16 servings

CREAM SHERRY CAKE

1 (18¼-ounce) box yellow butter cake mix
1 (3¼-ounce) box vanilla instant pudding mix
4 eggs
¾ cup oil
⅓ cup water
½ cup cream sherry
1 teaspoon cinnamon
1 cup finely chopped pecans

Preheat oven to 325 degrees. With mixer, combine cake mix, pudding mix, eggs, oil, water, cream sherry, and cinnamon. Pour into a greased Bundt pan coated with pecans. Bake for 50–60 minutes. Remove cake from oven. Pour hot Glaze over hot cake in pan, and let set in pan for 25 minutes before removing from pan.
Yield: 12–16 servings

GLAZE:
½ stick margarine
½ cup sugar
¼ cup water
¼ cup cream sherry

In a saucepan, combine margarine, sugar, and water; boil 2 minutes. Add cream sherry and boil for 2 minutes.

Fig Preserve Cake

Coconut Pound Cake

COCONUT POUND CAKE

This grand-prize recipe contest winner had people selling the sought-after mix on ebay.

1 (18¼-ounce) box coconut supreme cake mix
²/₃ cup sugar
²/₃ cup oil
1 cup sour cream
4 eggs
½ teaspoon vanilla
Confectioners' sugar (optional)

Preheat oven to 350 degrees. With mixer, combine cake mix and sugar. Add oil, sour cream, eggs, and vanilla; beat 2 minutes. Pour batter into greased and floured heavy Bundt pan, and bake 45 minutes. Do not open the oven; turn oven off and leave cake in oven 1 hour. Remove cake from oven. Remove cake from pan; cool on wire rack. May dust with confectioners' sugar, if desired.
Yield: 12–16 servings

CREAM CHEESE POUND CAKE

This is my favorite pound cake.

2 sticks unsalted butter, softened
1 stick margarine, softened
1 (8-ounce) package cream cheese, softened
3 cups sugar
6 eggs
3 cups all-purpose flour
1 tablespoon vanilla

Preheat oven to 325 degrees. With mixer, cream butter, margarine, cream cheese, and sugar; mix until smooth. Alternate adding eggs and flour, beginning and ending with flour, and beating well after each addition. Add vanilla, and mix thoroughly. Pour into a well-greased and lightly floured large Bundt or tube pan, and bake for 90 minutes or until done. Cool in pan for 10 minutes and remove.
Yield: 16–20 servings

AMARETTO POUND CAKE

2 sticks unsalted butter
½ cup solid shortening
3 cups sugar
5 large eggs, room temperature
¹/₃ cup amaretto
3 cups all-purpose flour
¹/₈ teaspoon salt
½ teaspoon baking powder
1 cup milk

Preheat oven to 325 degrees. With mixer, cream butter, shortening, and sugar until light and fluffy. Beat in eggs, one at a time. Beat in amaretto. Sift together flour, salt, and baking powder. Add milk and flour alternately, beginning and ending with flour mixture. Pour into greased and floured Bundt or tube pan, and bake for 1 hour and 25 minutes. Cool in pan on wire rack. Turn cake onto plate and poke holes in the top with a toothpick. Pour Glaze into holes and drizzle on side of cake.
Yield: 16–20 servings

GLAZE:
1 cup sugar
½ cup water
¹/₃ cup amaretto

In a small saucepan, combine ingredients and heat to boiling. Stir until sugar dissolves.

SUSAN'S BUTTERSCOTCH CAKE

1 (18-ounce) box French vanilla cake mix
1 (3¼-ounce) box vanilla instant pudding mix
⅔ cup sugar
3 tablespoons all-purpose flour
½ cup oil
1 cup sour cream
4 eggs
⅓ cup DeKuyper Buttershots liqueur
1 (6-ounce) package butterscotch chips
½ cup each: chopped pecans and shredded
    coconut (optional)

Preheat oven to 350 degrees. With mixer, combine cake mix, pudding, sugar, and flour. Add oil, sour cream, eggs, and liqueur, and beat for 3 minutes on medium speed. Fold in chips. Stir in pecans and coconut, if desired. Pour into a well-greased and floured tube or Bundt pan. Bake for 45 minutes, then turn oven off. Do not open oven. Leave in oven for 1 hour. Remove to wire rack.
Yield: 12–16 servings

LEMON SUPREME CAKE

1 (18¼-ounce) box lemon supreme cake mix
½ cup sugar
½ cup oil
1 cup apricot nectar
4 eggs

Preheat oven to 350 degrees. With mixer, blend ingredients. Beat at medium speed for 2 minutes. Pour into greased and floured pan. Bake 35–40 minutes. Cool 5 minutes in pan on wire rack; remove from pan. Finish cooling on a rack. Drizzle Glaze over cake.
Yield: 12–16 servings

GLAZE:
1 cup confectioners' sugar, sifted
2 tablespoons lemon juice

Combine ingredients until smooth.

APPLE CAKE WITH CARAMEL

2 cups sugar
1½ cups vegetable oil
4 eggs
3 cups all-purpose flour
½ teaspoon salt
1 teaspoon baking soda
2 teaspoons ground cinnamon
1 teaspoon vanilla
1 cup chopped walnuts
3 apples, peeled and diced
1 (12-ounce) jar caramel topping

Preheat oven to 350 degrees. Beat sugar, oil, and eggs together. Add flour, salt, baking soda, and cinnamon. Batter will be stiff. Add vanilla, walnuts, and apples. Pour into a greased and floured 10-inch tube or Bundt pan. Bake for one hour and 10 minutes. Cool. Pour topping over cake.
Yield: 12–16 servings

ICED PUMPKIN BABY CAKES

1 (14-ounce) box Pillsbury Pumpkin Quick Bread
    mix
1½ teaspoons cinnamon
For garnish: lemon rind and lemon curls

Prepare mix according to muffin directions, adding cinnamon. Pour batter into a greased and floured small Bundt pans. Bake according to directions, testing for doneness with a toothpick. Allow cakes to cool on a wire rack for about 5 minutes before turning out of pan. Pour Icing over cakes, letting it drip down sides. Garnish with lemon rind and lemon curls.
Yield: 6 small Bundt cakes

ICING:
1 (12-ounce) can buttercream frosting
Zest and juice of 1 lemon

Beat ingredients until well blended.

YELLOW CUPCAKES WITH VANILLA FROSTING

3 cups cake flour
1¾ cups sugar
1 tablespoon baking powder
1 teaspoon salt
½ cup shortening
2 eggs
1 cup milk
1 teaspoon vanilla
1 teaspoon butter flavoring

Preheat oven to 350 degrees. Sift together flour, sugar, baking powder, and salt into mixing bowl. With mixer, beat in shortening, eggs, milk, vanilla, and butter flavoring for 4 minutes. Line 24 muffin cups with paper liners; fill ⅔ full with batter. Bake for 20 minutes. Remove from pans and cool on wire racks. Ice with Vanilla Frosting.
Yield: 24 regular or 48 mini cupcakes

VANILLA FROSTING:

1 stick margarine, softened
1 pound package of confectioners' sugar, sifted
¼ cup milk
1½ teaspoons vanilla

With mixer, beat margarine. Add sugar alternately with milk. Stir in vanilla. Add additional sugar or milk to reach desired consistency.

WHITE CUPCAKES WITH BUTTERCREAM FROSTING

1 (18¼-ounce) box white cake mix
¼ teaspoon almond extract

Preheat oven to 350 degrees. Prepare cake mix according to directions, and add almond extract. Pour ⅔ full into greased muffin or mini muffin pans. Bake according to package directions; do not brown top. Remove to rack; cool. Ice with Buttercream Frosting.
Yield: 24 regular cupcakes or 48 mini cupcakes

VANILLA BUTTERCREAM FROSTING:

1 cup shortening, softened
⅛ teaspoon salt
¾ teaspoon butter flavoring
¼ teaspoon almond extract
½ cup water
1 (2-pound) bag confectioners' sugar

With mixer, beat shortening and salt until fluffy. Combine flavorings with water. Add sugar alternately with water mixture to shortening while mixing.

CHOCOLATE BUTTERCREAM FROSTING:

3 sticks unsalted butter, softened
2 tablespoons milk
9 ounces semisweet chocolate, melted
1 teaspoon vanilla
¼ teaspoon almond extract
2¾ cups confectioners' sugar

With mixer, beat butter until creamy. Add milk, slightly cooled chocolate, and flavorings. Beat in sugar.

STRAWBERRY CUPCAKES

1 (18¼-ounce) box white cake mix

1 (3-ounce) package strawberry gelatin

1 cup oil

½ cup milk

4 eggs

1 cup frozen strawberries, thawed and drained

1 cup finely chopped pecans

1 cup grated coconut

Preheat oven to 350 degrees. With mixer, combine ingredients; pour into mini muffin pans with liners. Fill ⅔ full. Bake 8–10 minutes. Cool and ice with Strawberry Icing.
Yield: 36–40 mini cupcakes

STRAWBERRY ICING:

1 stick margarine, softened

1 (8-ounce) package cream cheese, softened

1 pound confectioners' sugar

1 teaspoon vanilla

½ cup frozen strawberries, thawed and drained

½ cup finely chopped pecans

½ cup grated coconut

With mixer, beat margarine and cream cheese until smooth. Add sugar, vanilla, and strawberries; mix well. Stir in pecans and coconut.

LEMONADE CUPCAKES

These cupcakes are so light made from an angel food cake mix.

1 (16-ounce) box angel food cake mix

¾ cup water

½ cup frozen lemonade

For garnish: crushed lemon drop or Lemonhead candies

Prepare cake mix according to package directions for cupcakes, and add water and lemonade. Ice with Lemon Frosting and garnish with crushed lemon drops or Lemonheads.

LEMON FROSTING:

1 (8-ounce) package cream cheese, softened

1 stick butter, softened

3 cups confectioners' sugar

Zest and juice of 1 lemon

With mixer, beat all ingredients together until light and fluffy.

ESPRESSO CUPCAKES

1 (18¼-ounce) box chocolate cake mix

2 tablespoons espresso powder

1 tablespoon water

For garnish: chocolate covered espresso beans

Prepare cake mix according to directions for cupcakes, and add espresso powder dissolved in water. Cool and ice with Coffee Cream Frosting.

COFFEE CREAM FROSTING:

4 ounces cream cheese, softened

2 tablespoons unsalted butter, softened

¼ cup strong coffee, cooled

½ teaspoon vanilla

2 cups confectioners' sugar, sifted

With mixer, beat cream cheese, butter, coffee, and vanilla until smooth. Beat in sugar.

TOASTED COCONUT CUPCAKES

1 (18¼-ounce) box coconut supreme cake mix
1 cup toasted flaked coconut

Prepare cake mix according to directions for cupcakes. Cool and ice with Seafoam Icing, and sprinkle with toasted coconut.
Yield: 24 cupcakes

SEAFOAM ICING:
¾ cup sugar
2 egg whites
2 teaspoons water
⅛ teaspoon cream of tartar
½ teaspoon vanilla

In top of double boiler, combine sugar, egg whites, water, and cream of tartar. Over simmering water, beat with a hand mixer until mixture reaches 160 degrees on candy thermometer. Remove from heat, add vanilla, and beat at medium speed until soft peaks form.

CARROT CUPCAKES

With a mix, these cupcakes are quickly prepared.

1 (18¼-ounce) box carrot cake mix
½ cup chopped pecans
For garnish: fresh carrot curls

Prepare cake mix according to directions for cupcakes, and stir in pecans. Cool, and ice with Cream Cheese Frosting. Garnish with carrot curls.
Yield: 24 cupcakes

CREAM CHEESE FROSTING:
1 stick unsalted butter, softened
1 (8-ounce) package cream cheese, softened
6 cups confectioners' sugar
2 teaspoons lemon juice

With mixer, beat butter and cream cheese until fluffy. Beat in sugar and lemon juice.

Espresso Cupcakes, Toasted Coconut Cupcakes, and Carrot Cupcakes

PIES

BUTTERY PECAN PIE

½ cup light corn syrup

½ cup dark corn syrup

3 eggs

½ cup sugar

½ cup Splenda Brown Sugar Blend

2 tablespoons unsalted butter, melted

1 teaspoon vanilla

½ teaspoon butter flavoring

2 tablespoons DeKuyper Buttershots liqueur

1½ cups chopped pecans

1 (9-inch) pie crust, unbaked

Preheat oven to 350 degrees. In large bowl, combine light corn syrup, dark corn syrup, eggs, sugar, brown sugar, melted butter, vanilla, butter flavoring, and Buttershots liqueur. With mixer on medium speed, combine. Add pecans and blend thoroughly. Pour into unbaked pie shell. Bake for 55–60 minutes. Cool for 2 hours. Yield: 1 pie

CARAMEL PECAN PIE

36 caramels, unwrapped

¼ cup water

½ stick butter, cubed

3 eggs

¾ cup sugar

1 teaspoon Madagascar Bourbon vanilla

⅛ teaspoon salt

1⅓ cups chopped pecans, toasted

1 (9-inch) deep-dish pie shell, unbaked

½ cup pecan halves, not toasted

Preheat oven to 350 degrees. In saucepan over low heat, combine caramels, water, and butter, stirring continually until melted; set aside. Beat eggs, sugar, vanilla, and salt until smooth. Gradually add caramel mixture; stir in toasted pecans. Pour filling into pastry shell. Arrange untoasted pecan halves around edges over filling. Bake for 35–40 minutes or until set. Cool on wire rack. Yield: 1 pie

Buttery Pecan Pie

CHESS PIE

3 eggs
1½ cups sugar
⅓ cup buttermilk
1 stick margarine, melted
1½ cups grated coconut
1 teaspoon vanilla
1 (9-inch) pie crust, unbaked

Preheat oven to 350 degrees. Beat eggs; stir in sugar. Stir in buttermilk, margarine, coconut, and vanilla. Pour into pie shell and bake 30 minutes or until set.
Yield: 1 pie

SWEET POTATO PIE

This is my grandmother's recipe.

2 cups sweet potatoes, boiled and mashed
1 cup sugar
1 stick butter, melted
2 eggs, beaten
½ cup milk
1 cup grated coconut
1 teaspoon vanilla
1 (9-inch) pie crust, unbaked

Preheat oven to 350 degrees. Combine all ingredients, and spoon into a pie crust. Place on a cookie sheet, and bake for 45 minutes or until set.
Yield: 1 pie

PUMPKIN PIE

This is the ultimate Thanksgiving pumpkin pie.

1 (15-ounce) can pumpkin
3 eggs, beaten
1 cup sugar
¼ teaspoon each: cloves and ginger
1½ teaspoons cinnamon
¼ teaspoon salt
1 (5-ounce) can evaporated milk
2 (9-inch) pie crusts, unbaked
1 (18¼-ounce) box yellow cake mix
1 cup chopped pecans
1 stick butter, melted, divided
½ pint heavy cream
¼ cup confectioners' sugar
For garnish: cinnamon

Preheat oven to 350 degrees. With mixer on low, combine pumpkin, eggs, sugar, spices, and milk; pour half into each pie crust. Mix cake mix and pecans, and divide in half. Sprinkle half on each pie. Drizzle ½ stick melted butter on each pie. Bake on a cookie sheet for 45 minutes. With mixer, beat cream; add confectioners' sugar. Spoon on pie and sprinkle with cinnamon.
Yield: 2 pies

BLUEBERRY PIE

4½ cups fresh blueberries
½ cup sugar
1⅓ cups all-purpose flour, divided
½ teaspoon cinnamon
1 tablespoon lemon juice
1 (9-inch) deep-dish pie crust, unbaked

TOPPING:

1 stick margarine, softened
½ cup brown sugar

Preheat oven to 400 degrees. Combine blueberries, sugar, ⅓ cup flour, cinnamon, and lemon juice, and pour into pie crust; set aside. Combine margarine, remaining 1 cup flour, and brown sugar. Crumble on top of blueberries. Bake 30 minutes; remove and cover with foil. Bake 20 minutes. Remove to wire rack. Serve with ice cream or whipped topping.
Yield: 1 pie

PEACH TARTS

8 tart shells, or 1 (9-inch) pie crust, unbaked
10–12 fresh peaches, pitted, peeled, and diced
1 cup sugar
1 egg, beaten
⅓ cup all-purpose flour
1 teaspoon vanilla
1 teaspoon almond extract
4½ tablespoons butter, melted

Preheat oven to 350 degrees. Combine peaches and sugar and place in tart shells or pie crust. Stir together egg and flour. Add flavorings. Crumble mixture over peaches. Drizzle with butter. Bake for 40 minutes. Serve warm with ice cream.
Yield: 8 tarts or 1 pie

APPLE TURNOVERS

These are the perfect hand pies.

3 Granny Smith apples, peeled and diced
1 teaspoon grated orange zest
3 tablespoons freshly squeezed orange juice
4 tablespoons dried cherries
3 tablespoons sugar, plus extra to sprinkle on top
1 tablespoon all-purpose flour
1 teaspoon ground cinnamon
⅛ teaspoon salt
1 (17.3-ounce) package frozen puff pastry
1 egg, beaten with 1 tablespoon water
1 cup caramel topping
For garnish: vanilla ice cream and caramel topping

Preheat oven to 400 degrees. Toss apples with orange zest and juice; add cherries, sugar, flour, cinnamon, and salt. On a floured board, lightly roll out each sheet of puff pastry to a 12x12-inch square. Cut each sheet into 4 squares. Brush the edges of each square with the egg wash, and place ⅓ cup apple mixture on each square. Fold pastry diagonally over the apple mixture and seal edges with fork. Place on pan lined with parchment paper. Brush tops with egg wash and sprinkle with sugar. Cut 2 small slits in top of each turnover and bake for 20 minutes, until brown and puffed. Serve warm or at room temperature with vanilla ice cream and drizzle of caramel topping.
Yield: 8 turnovers

APPLE PIE

1½ (15-ounce) packages rolled pie crusts
3 tablespoons butter
1 cup light packed brown sugar
½ teaspoon cornstarch
6 Granny Smith apples, peeled and sliced
1 teaspoon each: vanilla and cinnamon
1 egg, beaten
2 tablespoons sugar

Preheat oven to 375 degrees. Place one pie crust in bottom of 9-inch pie plate; set aside. In saucepan over medium heat, combine butter, brown sugar, cornstarch, apples, vanilla, and cinnamon; cook 10 minutes. Pour into pie crust, and top with second crust, crimping edges and cutting 4 slits in top. Edge pie with leaves cut with cookie cutter from remaining pie crust. Brush with egg, and sprinkle with sugar. Cover edge of pie with foil. Bake 50 minutes.
Yield: 1 pie

APPLE CRUMB PIE

1 (21-ounce) can sliced apples, chopped
½ cup sugar
2 teaspoons cinnamon
1 (9-inch) pie crust, unbaked
1 stick margarine, cold
½ cup sugar
¾ cup all-purpose flour

Preheat oven to 450 degrees. Mix together apples, sugar, and cinnamon. Place mixture in pie crust. Combine margarine, sugar, and flour; crumble on top of apple mixture. Bake 15 minutes; reduce heat to 350 degrees, and bake for 30 minutes. Serve with ice cream, if desired.
Yield: 1 pie

Apple Pie

BROWNIE PIE

This pie can also be doubled to bake in a 9x13-inch pan, then cut into shapes.

1 stick margarine, melted
1 cup sugar
2 tablespoons cocoa
2 eggs
½ cup all-purpose flour
1 cup chopped pecans
1 teaspoon vanilla
1 (9-inch) pie crust, unbaked
For garnish: vanilla ice cream and chocolate sauce

Preheat oven to 350 degrees. Cream margarine, sugar, and cocoa. Stir in eggs and flour. Add pecans and vanilla. Pour into crust. Bake for 30 minutes. Serve with ice cream and chocolate sauce.
Yield: 1 pie

FUDGE PIE

1½ cups sugar
1 stick margarine, melted
3 tablespoons cocoa
2 eggs
½ cup evaporated milk
1 tablespoon vanilla
1 (9-inch) pie crust, unbaked
1 (8-ounce) container whipped topping
For garnish: shaved chocolate

Preheat oven to 400 degrees. Stir together sugar, margarine, and cocoa. Mix in eggs, milk, and vanilla. Pour into crust and bake for 10 minutes. Reduce heat to 350 degrees and bake for 25 minutes. Serve with whipped topping. Garnish with shaved chocolate.
Yield: 1 pie

HERSHEY BAR PIE

6 (41-gram) Hershey's chocolate bars with almonds
16 marshmallows
½ cup milk
2 cups heavy cream, divided
1 (9-inch) pie crust, baked
¼ cup confectioners' sugar

In a double boiler, melt candy bars, marshmallows, and milk; cool. With mixer, beat 1 cup cream until stiff; fold into chocolate mixture. Pour into crust and chill. With mixer, beat remaining cream; beat in sugar. Serve pie with whipped cream.
Yield: 1 pie

BUTTERSCOTCH TART

½ (15-ounce) package rolled pie crust
½ cup firmly packed brown sugar
½ cup sugar
½ cup all-purpose flour
1 stick butter, melted
¼ cup dark corn syrup
3 large eggs
1 cup butterscotch chips
1 cup chopped pecans, toasted
For garnish: vanilla ice cream, and butterscotch topping

Preheat oven to 350 degrees. On lightly floured surface, unroll pie crust. Roll pastry into a 12-inch circle. Press pie crust into a 9-inch tart pan. In a medium bowl, combine sugars and flour. Whisk in melted butter, corn syrup, and eggs until mixture is smooth. Stir in butterscotch chips and pecans. Spoon mixture into prepared pie crust. Bake for 40–45 minutes, or until center is set; cool 30 minutes before cutting. Serve warm with ice cream and butterscotch topping.
Yield: 1 tart

LIME MERINGUE PIE

1 cup fresh raspberries

1½ cups sugar, divided

3 egg yolks

1 (14-ounce) can sweetened condensed milk

½ cup Key lime juice

Zest of 1 lime

1 (9-inch) pie crust, baked lightly

3 egg whites

2 tablespoons corn syrup

⅛ teaspoon salt

¼ cup water

Preheat oven to 350 degrees. Combine raspberries and ½ cup sugar; set aside. Whisk together egg yolks, milk, lime juice, and zest. Pour into crust and bake 12 minutes. Remove from oven and raise temperature to 450 degrees.

For meringue, beat egg whites until soft peaks form; set aside. In a saucepan over medium heat, stir together remaining 1 cup sugar, corn syrup, salt, and water. When sugar is dissolved, bring to a boil, and heat over medium high for 6–8 minutes. Slowly pour into egg whites and beat for 4 minutes until meringue is firm. Spread over center of pie, leaving a 1-inch border around the outside edge. Bake for 3–5 minutes until lightly browned. Chill for at least 3 hours, and serve with berries tucked under the edge of meringue.

Yield: 1 pie

PEACHES AND CREAM TARTS

3 fresh peaches, pitted, peeled, and chopped
¼ cup light brown sugar, packed
8 tart shells, or 1 (9-inch) pie crust, baked
1 (8-ounce) package cream cheese, softened
2 tablespoons sugar
2 tablespoons half-and-half
2 cups whipped topping, divided
1 (3¼-ounce) box vanilla instant pudding
1 cup cold milk
1 teaspoon almond extract
For garnish: whipped topping, sliced peaches, fresh
    mint, and toasted sliced almonds

Stir peaches with brown sugar, and spread in bottom of tart shells or pie crust. With mixer, beat cream cheese and sugar. Add half-and-half, and fold in whipped topping. Spoon on top of peaches. Prepare pudding with milk; add almond extract. Spread over cream cheese layer. Chill overnight. Serve with whipped topping and garnish with peach slices, mint, and sliced almonds. Yield: 8 tarts or 1 pie

PRALINE KEY LIME PIE

½ stick unsalted butter
½ cup chopped pecans
½ cup packed light brown sugar
1 (9-inch) graham cracker pie crust
6 egg yolks
1½ (14-ounce) cans sweetened condensed milk
⅓ cup Key lime juice
1 cup heavy cream
¼ cup confectioners' sugar

Preheat oven to 350 degrees. In saucepan, melt butter and stir in pecans; cook 2 minutes. Add sugar; melt until smooth. Bring to a boil, and remove from heat. Pour over bottom of crust. Whisk together yolks, milk, and juice. Pour over praline layer. Bake 12 minutes. Cool and chill. With mixer, beat cream until stiff; gradually beat in sugar. Spread on pie. Yield: 1 pie

STRAWBERRY CREAM PIE

½ cup packed brown sugar
1 stick butter, room temperature
1 cup all-purpose flour
½ cup chopped almonds
2 egg whites
1 cup sugar
2 teaspoons lemon juice
1 (10-ounce) package frozen strawberries, thawed
1 cup heavy cream, whipped
For garnish: fresh strawberries and mint

Preheat oven to 350 degrees. For crust and topping, combine brown sugar, butter, flour, and almonds. Place on foil-lined cookie sheet, and bake 15–20 minutes. Cool and crumble. Press ¾ of mixture in the bottom of a greased 9-inch pie plate. For filling, with mixer, beat egg whites, sugar, and lemon juice until soft peaks form. Stir in strawberries. Fold in whipped cream. Pour into crust, and top with remaining crumb mixture. Freeze. Thaw 10 minutes before serving. Garnish with strawberries and mint. Yield: 1 pie

CINNAMON LEMON PIE

The cinnamon graham crackers give this pie a special flavor.

6 cinnamon graham crackers, finely crushed
2 tablespoons butter, melted
1 (14-ounce) can sweetened condensed milk
2 egg yolks
½ cup freshly squeezed lemon juice
1 tablespoon lemon zest
For garnish: whipped topping, lemon curls, and lemon zest

Preheat oven to 350 degrees. Combine crumbs and add butter. Press crumbs into 9-inch pie plate and chill. Combine condensed milk and egg yolks; mix until smooth. Stir in lemon juice and zest. Pour into prepared crust. Bake for 20 minutes. Cool and chill. Garnish with whipped topping, lemon curls, and lemon zest.
Yield: 1 pie

LEMON PAVLOVAS WITH BERRIES

4 egg whites
1¼ cups sugar, divided
¼ teaspoon each: salt and cream of tartar
Zest of 2 lemons
½ cup each: raspberries and blackberries
Juice of 1 lemon
1 (8-ounce) container whipped topping
1 teaspoon vanilla

Preheat oven to 200 degrees. With mixer, beat egg whites until soft peaks form; gradually add 1 cup sugar, salt, cream of tartar, and zest. Beat to consistency of marshmallow crème. Spoon or pipe onto cookie sheet lined with parchment. With a spoon, create a well in center of each meringue. Bake 2 hours. Remove to wire rack. For berry sauce, combine berries with 2 tablespoons sugar and lemon juice; chill. Whisk together whipped topping, remaining 2 tablespoons sugar, and vanilla; chill. Serve meringues with whipped topping and berry sauce.
Yield: 6–8 meringues

Lemon Pavlovas with Berries

Cheesecake with Cherries and Chocolate

CREAMY DESSERTS

CHEESECAKE WITH CHERRIES AND CHOCOLATE

CRUST:

1 stick butter, melted
1½ cups graham cracker crumbs
⅓ cup confectioners' sugar
½ cup finely chopped pecans

Preheat oven to 350 degrees. Combine ingredients; mix well. Press into bottom of greased 10-inch springform pan.

FILLING:

3 (8-ounce) packages cream cheese, softened
2 cups sugar, divided
5 eggs
3 tablespoons lemon juice
1 (21-ounce) can cherry pie filling, divided
1 cup sour cream
1 teaspoon vanilla
For garnish: 1 (12-ounce) jar chocolate topping and white and dark chocolate covered cherries with stems

With mixer, beat cream cheese and 1½ cups sugar. Beat in eggs, one at a time; add lemon juice. Pour half into Crust. Layer ½ can cherry pie filling on top of cream cheese mixture, reserving remainder for garnish. Top with remaining half of cream cheese mixture. Bake 45 minutes. Remove from oven. Reduce oven to 300 degrees. Spread with sour cream combined with ½ cup sugar and vanilla. Bake 15 minutes. Cool and chill. Garnish with remaining ½ can cherry pie filling, chocolate topping, and chocolate covered cherries.
Yield: 1 cheesecake

For an impressive presentation, bake 2 cheesecakes of different sizes. Place larger cheesecake on plate and spread with remaining cherry pie filling, dripping down sides. Top with smaller cheesecake, and spread with chocolate topping, dripping down sides.

PEACHES 'N' CREAM CHEESECAKE

¾ cup all-purpose flour
1 teaspoon baking powder
1 (3¼-ounce) box vanilla instant pudding mix
3 tablespoons margarine, softened
1 egg
½ cup milk
1 (16-ounce) can sliced peaches
1 (8-ounce) package cream cheese, softened
½ cup plus 1½ teaspoons sugar, divided
¼ teaspoon ground cinnamon

Preheat oven to 350 degrees. With mixer, combine flour, baking powder, pudding mix, margarine, egg, and milk. Beat at medium speed until smooth. Pour mixture into a greased 8-inch round cake pan. Drain peaches, reserving 3 tablespoons liquid; set aside liquid. Arrange peach slices over batter. With mixer, combine cream cheese, ½ cup sugar, and reserved liquid. Beat 2 minutes at medium speed. Spoon mixture over peaches in center of cake, leaving a 1-inch border around edge of cake pan. Combine remaining 1½ teaspoons sugar and cinnamon; sprinkle over cream cheese filling. Bake for 35 minutes; remove from oven and cool at room temperature. Chill for several hours before serving.
Yield: 1 cheesecake

COCONUT CHEESECAKE

Who doesn't love coconut and berries with cheesecake?

3 tablespoons butter, melted
1²/₃ cups flaked coconut, toasted, divided
1 cup finely chopped pecans
3 (8-ounce) packages cream cheese, softened
1 cup sugar, divided
3 eggs
1 teaspoon vanilla, divided
¼ teaspoon almond extract
1 egg white

Preheat oven to 350 degrees. For crust, combine butter, 1 cup coconut, and pecans. Press into the bottom of a 9-inch springform pan; set aside.

For filling, with mixer, beat cream cheese and ½ cup sugar until smooth. Add eggs. Beat in ½ teaspoon vanilla, and almond extract. Pour over crust. Bake for 35 minutes. For topping, with mixer, beat egg white, remaining ½ cup sugar, and remaining ½ teaspoon vanilla until soft peaks form. Fold in remaining ²/₃ cup coconut. Spread over cheesecake, return to oven, and bake for 20 minutes. Cool on wire rack, cover, and chill for 4 hours before running a knife around edges, removing from pan, and serving. Yield: 1 cheesecake

CREAM CROWN

2 (3-ounce) packages ladyfingers
1 (8-ounce) package cream cheese, softened
½ cup sugar
2 cups whipping cream
1 teaspoon vanilla
2 tablespoons red currant jelly
1 tablespoon water
Fresh raspberries or fresh chopped strawberries
For garnish: lemon peeling curls

Lightly grease bottom of a 9-inch springform pan. Line the sides with half the ladyfingers, rounded sides out. With a mixer, beat cream cheese until creamy, about 1 minute. Gradually add sugar, and continue beating for 1 minute. In another bowl, combine cream and vanilla, and beat with mixer until soft peaks form; do not overbeat. Fold beaten cream into cream cheese mixture. Spread half of cheese filling in bottom of pan. Arrange remaining ladyfingers on top of filling. Top with remaining filling. Cover and chill overnight. Heat red currant jelly and water until dissolved; cool. Before serving, arrange berries on top, and drizzle with currant jelly glaze. Garnish with lemon curls.
Yield: 12 servings

LEMON CREAM CROWN:
Add 1 (3-ounce) package softened cream cheese and juice and zest of one lemon. Garnish with lemon peel curls and fresh mint.

GRAND MARNIER CROWN:
Add 1 (3-ounce) package softened cream cheese and 2 tablespoons of Grand Marnier. Garnish with orange peel curls and fresh mint.

FOR MINIATURE CROWNS:
Line mini springform pans with ladyfingers and layer filling and 2 ladyfingers for each pan.
Yield: 4 miniature crowns with one additional package of ladyfingers.

DEATH BY CHOCOLATE

1 (20-ounce) package brownie mix, baked
1 teaspoon sugar, dissolved in 4 tablespoons
    prepared black coffee
4 cups milk
3 (3¼-ounce) boxes instant chocolate pudding mix
8 (1¼-ounce) Heath candy bars, crushed
½ cup slivered almonds, toasted
1 (8-ounce) container whipped topping

Punch holes in brownies with a fork and pour
in sugar-coffee mixture. Crumble brownies; set
aside. With mixer, beat milk and pudding mixes
until thickened; set aside. Combine candy and
almonds. In individual dessert dishes, layer 1
tablespoon brownies, 3 tablespoons pudding,
1 tablespoon candy and almond pieces, and 1
tablespoon whipped topping. Repeat, and end
with whipped topping. Cover with plastic wrap,
and chill. To serve, sprinkle with candy and
almonds.
Yield: 16 servings

WHITE CHOCOLATE MOUSSE

An easy, decadent dessert!

1 (5-ounce) box white chocolate pudding mix
1 (8-ounce) package cream cheese, softened
1 (8-ounce) container whipped topping
For garnish: whipped topping and fresh berries

Prepare pudding mix as directed on package.
With mixer, beat cream cheese until fluffy; grad-
ually stir in pudding. Fold in whipped topping.
Pour into bowl or individual dishes. Garnish with
whipped topping and fresh berries.
Yield: 8 servings

LEMON CUSTARD

⅓ cup all-purpose flour
1 cup sugar
⅛ teaspoon salt
4 tablespoons butter, softened
4 eggs, separated
1 cup milk
3 tablespoons lemon juice
½ teaspoon lemon zest
For garnish: whipped cream, fresh raspberries, and
    mint

Sift together flour, sugar, and salt. With mixer,
cream butter and egg yolks into dry ingredients.
Beat in milk, lemon juice, and zest. Preheat
oven to 350 degrees. Beat egg whites until stiff
peaks form; fold into custard. Pour into buttered
custard cups. Place cups in a pan with about
1 inch of water, and bake for 40 minutes. Turn
custards out of cups, and serve with whipped
cream. Garnish with raspberries and mint.
Yield: 8 servings

 FLAN WITH PRALINE SAUCE

12 ounces cream cheese, softened
1 stick butter, softened
½ cup sour cream, room temperature
½ cup sugar
1 (¼-ounce) package unflavored gelatin
¼ cup cold water
For garnish: sugar cookies (thin work best)

With mixer, beat cream cheese, butter, and sour cream. Blend in sugar. Soften gelatin in cold water by dissolving over a bowl of hot water. Add to cream cheese mixture. Pour into greased 1-quart mold, or 8 individual ramekins or molds. Chill until firm. To serve, unmold onto a serving plate. Top with Praline Sauce. Garnish with cookies. May be frozen.
Yield: 6–8 servings

PRALINE SAUCE:

3 tablespoons butter
1 cup firmly packed brown sugar
½ cup half-and-half
1 cup chopped pecans
1 teaspoon vanilla

In heavy saucepan over low heat, melt butter. Add brown sugar. Stirring constantly, cook for 5–8 minutes or until mixture is smooth. Gradually stir in half-and-half. Cook for 1 minute; remove from heat. Stir in pecans and vanilla. Cool to room temperature. May be made ahead and refrigerated. Bring to room temperature before use.
Yield: 2 cups

CRÈME BRÛLÉE

2 cups heavy cream
1 large egg
4 large egg yolks
Pinch of salt
1 teaspoon vanilla
4 teaspoons sugar

In saucepan over medium heat, bring cream to a boil; remove from heat. Combine egg and yolks. Slowly whisk half hot cream into the eggs. When fully incorporated, add remaining cream and salt, whisking constantly. Add vanilla. Preheat oven to 300 degrees. Divide the custard between 4 ramekins. Place ramekins into baking pan; pour hot water in pan to come halfway up sides of ramekins. Place pan in the lower third of the oven, and bake 50 minutes until custards are just set. Remove ramekins from the baking dish, and cool 30–40 minutes. Cover with plastic wrap and chill for several hours or overnight.

Just before serving, sprinkle custards evenly with 1 teaspoon sugar for a complete, even coating. Caramelize sugar in one of the following ways and serve.
Yield: 4 servings

TO CARAMELIZE SUGAR:

With a blowtorch: Hold the flame about 2 inches from the sugar and slowly guide the flame back and forth across the surface of each custard until they are golden brown in color. The tops will harden as they cool.

In the oven: Place the oven rack about 2 inches from the heat source. Arrange custards on a cookie sheet, and with the broiler on high, broil until the sugar has melted and is golden brown in color. Watch the custards carefully, and move the baking sheet around if some are browning too quickly. The tops will harden as they cool.

WHITE CHOCOLATE BREAD PUDDING

6 eggs
1½ cups sugar
2 pints half-and-half
¼ teaspoon salt
2 teaspoons vanilla
8 dinner rolls, torn into bite-size pieces
1½ cups white chocolate chips
2 tablespoons butter, softened
½ cup brown sugar
For garnish: white chocolate curls and raspberries

Preheat oven to 350 degrees. Whisk eggs, sugar, half-and-half, salt, and vanilla together. Fold in rolls, and add white chocolate chips. Pour into a greased 9x13-inch baking dish. Bake for 1 hour. Combine butter and brown sugar. Remove from oven and sprinkle with butter and brown sugar. Serve warm with ice cream and garnish with raspberries and chocolate curls.
Yield: 12–16 servings

 LIME FREEZE

This dessert can be made with lemons or limes.

1 stick plus 2 tablespoons margarine, melted and
  divided
1 cup finely chopped pecans
1½ cups finely crumbled vanilla wafers
1 (8-ounce) package cream cheese, softened
1 cup confectioners' sugar
1 teaspoon lime flavoring
4 tablespoons lime zest, divided
1 (12-ounce) container whipped topping
6 tablespoons cornstarch
1½ cups sugar
½ teaspoon salt
1¼ cups water
Few drops green food coloring
⅔ cup freshly squeezed lime juice
For garnish: whipped topping, fresh mint, and
  lime zest

Preheat oven to 475 degrees. Combine 1 stick margarine, pecans, and crumbs with a pastry blender until texture of cornmeal. Pat into bottom of a greased 9x13-inch pan. Bake 7 minutes; cool. With mixer, beat cream cheese, confectioners' sugar, lime flavoring, and 2 tablespoons zest until smooth. Fold in whipped topping, and spread over the crumb layer. Freeze about 1 hour. For sauce, bring cornstarch, sugar, salt, and water to a boil. Reduce heat to low and cook until thickened. Remove from heat, and add remaining 2 tablespoons margarine, remaining 2 tablespoons zest, and food coloring; cool. When cooled, add lime juice and stir until smooth. Spread on top of cream cheese layer, and return to freezer until ready to serve. Cut into small squares or circles, and garnish with whipped topping, mint, and lime zest.
Yield: 12–16 servings

EASY HOMEMADE VANILLA ICE CREAM

This is the easiest and most delicious homemade ice cream.

2 (14-ounce) cans sweetened condensed milk
1 (12-ounce) can evaporated milk
¾ cup sugar
2 teaspoons vanilla
Milk

Combine condensed and evaporated milks, sugar, and vanilla. Add milk to make 1 gallon. Freeze according to ice cream maker instructions.
Yield: 1 gallon

CHOCOLATE ICE CREAM

½ gallon Dutch chocolate milk
2 (14-ounce) cans sweetened condensed milk
1 teaspoon vanilla

Combine ingredients. Freeze according to ice cream maker instructions.
Yield: 1 gallon

COFFEE ICE CREAM

2 (14-ounce) cans sweetened condensed milk
1 (12-ounce) can evaporated milk
¾ cup sugar
1 teaspoon vanilla
2¼ cups cold strong coffee
¼ cup Kahlúa
Half-and-half

Combine milks, sugar, vanilla coffee, and Kahlúa. Add half-and-half to make 1 gallon. Freeze according to ice cream maker instructions.
Yield: 1 gallon

CHERRY VANILLA ICE CREAM

3 (14-ounce) cans sweetened condensed milk
2 (12-ounce) cans evaporated milk
2 cups heavy cream
1 (10-ounce) jar maraschino cherries, chopped, with juice
3 tablespoons vanilla
Milk

Combine milks, cream, cherries, juice, and vanilla. Pour into canister of 6-quart ice cream freezer. Add milk to fill. Freeze according to ice cream maker instructions.
Yield: 6 quarts

PEACH ICE CREAM

1 (16-ounce) bag frozen peaches, thawed
4 cups half-and-half
1 (14-ounce) can sweetened condensed milk
1 tablespoon vanilla
2 teaspoons almond extract
1 teaspoon salt

In food processor, purée peaches. Whisk peach purée, half-and-half, flavorings, and salt. Chill overnight. Freeze according to ice cream maker instructions. For harder ice cream, pour into covered container, and place in freezer for a few hours.
Yield: 2 quarts

WATERMELON GRANITA

5 cups seeded and chopped watermelon
Juice from 1 lime

In food processor, pulse watermelon and lime juice. Pour into 8x8-inch glass dish; freeze. With a fork, scrape surface every 2 hours for 6 hours.
Yield: 6–8 servings

MEYER LEMON SHERBET IN LEMON CUPS

LEMON CUPS:
6 Meyer lemons
1 egg white
½ cup sugar

Cut a small sliver of skin from the bottoms of each lemon, allowing to stand flat. Cut ¼ off the top of each lemon, and scoop out insides, reserving juice for sherbet. With whisk, beat egg white until frothy. Brush egg white over lemons; roll in sugar. Freeze.

MEYER LEMON SHERBET:
½ cup Meyer lemon juice
½ cup heavy cream
½ cup milk
⅓ cup sugar
1 teaspoon vanilla
Zest of 2 Meyer lemons

In a saucepan, combine juice, cream, milk, sugar, and vanilla; cook for 8 minutes. Remove from heat; add zest. Chill in covered container for several hours. Freeze according to ice cream maker directions. Spoon into Lemon Cups. Yield: 6 servings

TREATS

BARS, COOKIES, AND CANDIES

Petit Fours and
Chocolate Brownie Bites

PETIT FOURS

1 (18¼-ounce) box white cake mix
¼ teaspoon almond extract
1 (12-ounce) can buttercream frosting

Preheat oven to 350 degrees. Prepare cake mix according to package directions, and add almond extract. Pour into a greased 10½x15½-inch jellyroll pan. Bake 17–20 minutes; do not brown top. Remove to wire rack and cover with wax paper; pat to adhere. In 5 minutes, remove wax paper and crust. Cool, cover with wax paper, and turn onto wax paper-lined rack. Freeze cake. Remove from freezer, remove wax paper, and frost with a thin layer of buttercream frosting. Trim edges, and cut into 1½-inch squares. Ice with Fondant Icing spooned over squares placed on wire rack over wax paper.
Yield: 60 petit fours

FONDANT ICING:

⅞ cup milk
3 tablespoons shortening
⅛ teaspoon salt
1½ teaspoons clear butter flavoring
1½ teaspoons clear vanilla
⅛ teaspoon almond extract
1 (2-pound) bag confectioners' sugar

Combine milk, shortening, and salt; microwave on LOW until melted. Pour into mixing bowl, and add flavorings. With mixer, beat in sugar until light and fluffy. Thin with warm milk, if needed.

CHOCOLATE BROWNIE BITES

1 (6-ounce) package semisweet chocolate chips
2 sticks unsalted butter
5 eggs
2½ cups sugar
2 teaspoons vanilla
1 cup all-purpose flour
⅛ teaspoon salt

Preheat oven to 325 degrees. In microwave, melt chocolate and butter; cool. With mixer, beat eggs and sugar until frothy. Stir in vanilla and chocolate mixture; then add flour and salt. Pour into greased 10½x15½-inch baking pan; bake 20–25 minutes, until toothpick comes out clean. Pour Icing over warm brownies. Cool before slicing.
Yield: 36 brownies

ICING:

1 (1-pound) box confectioners' sugar
1 stick butter
3 tablespoons cocoa
⅓ cup milk
1 teaspoon vanilla
1 cup chopped pecans

In saucepan over medium heat, stir together confectioners' sugar, butter, cocoa, and milk until smooth. Remove from heat; stir in vanilla and pecans.

EASY BROWNIES

1 (20-ounce) package brownie mix
1 cup each: sour cream, milk chocolate chips, and chopped pecans
1 (12-ounce) can chocolate icing
1 cup sugar

Preheat oven to 325 degrees. Mix brownies according to directions. Add sour cream, chocolate chips, and pecans. Spread into a 12x16x1-inch jellyroll pan lined with nonstick foil. Bake 15–18 minutes. Remove and ice. Cut into squares and dip bottoms into sugar.
Yield: 48 brownies

 FIG SQUARES

2 sticks butter, softened

1 cup sugar

2 egg yolks

2 cups all-purpose flour, sifted

2½ tablespoons cornstarch

¼ teaspoon salt

1 cup chopped pecans

1½ cups fig preserves, drained and chopped

Preheat oven to 325 degrees. With mixer, cream butter and sugar. Add egg yolks and beat until fluffy. Sift flour, cornstarch, and salt together. Add slowly to butter mixture; mix well and stir in pecans. Press half of the dough in the bottom and up the side of a greased 9x13-inch dish. Cover dough with fig preserves. Place remaining dough mixture on top of preserves in small pieces making a solid layer. Bake for 40–50 minutes, until lightly golden. Cool on wire rack.
Yield: 24 squares

BROWN SUGAR BARS

⅔ cup butter, softened

2 cups packed brown sugar

2 eggs

2 cups all-purpose flour

1 teaspoon vanilla

½ teaspoon salt

½ teaspoon baking soda

1 (6-ounce) package chocolate chips

Preheat oven to 350 degrees. Mix all ingredients except chocolate chips. Pour into a buttered 10½x15½-inch pan. Sprinkle with chocolate chips. Bake 20 minutes.
Yield: 36 bars

LEMON BARS

1½ cups graham cracker crumbs

5 tablespoons butter, melted

1½ (14-ounce) cans sweetened condensed milk

6 egg yolks

⅓ cup lemon juice

½ cup confectioners' sugar

Preheat oven to 350 degrees. For crust, combine cracker crumbs and melted butter. Press into greased 9x9-inch pan. For filling, stir together milk, yolks, and lemon juice. Pour filling over crust, and bake 12 minutes. Cool, and chill overnight. Sprinkle with confectioners' sugar.
Yield: 16 large or 81 small squares

SNICKERS CHESS BARS

1 (18¼-ounce) box yellow cake mix

½ cup packed light brown sugar

1 stick unsalted butter, melted

2 eggs

2 (2-ounce) Snickers bars, cut into small chunks

¾ cup dry roasted peanuts

2 ounces chocolate chips, melted

Preheat oven to 350 degrees. Combine cake mix and brown sugar. Add butter and eggs, and mix well. Stir in Snickers and peanuts. Press dough into greased 9x13-inch pan, and bake for 20-25 minutes. Cool, and drizzle with melted chips.
Yield: 24 bars

RASPBERRY CRUNCH BARS

1½ sticks butter, softened
1¼ cups quick-cooking oats
1 cup all-purpose flour
1⅓ cups sugar, divided
½ cup packed brown sugar
1 cup flaked coconut
1 cup chopped almonds
1 cup raspberry jam
1 (8-ounce) package cream cheese, softened
1 egg, beaten
½ cup sliced almonds

Preheat oven to 350 degrees. Combine butter, oats, flour, 1 cup sugar, brown sugar, coconut, and chopped almonds. Reserve 1½ cups, and press remainder into ungreased 9x13-inch pan. Bake 15 minutes; cool 5 minutes, and spread with jam. With mixer, cream remaining ⅓ cup sugar and cream cheese. Add egg, and pour over jam. Sprinkle with reserved crumb mixture. Sprinkle with sliced almonds. Bake 20–25 minutes.
Yield: 36 bars

CARAMEL BROWNIES

1 (14-ounce) package light caramels, unwrapped
⅔ cup evaporated milk, divided
1 (18¼-ounce) box German chocolate cake mix
1½ sticks margarine, melted
1 cup chopped pecans
1 (16-ounce) package chocolate chips

Preheat oven to 350 degrees. In microwave on LOW heat, melt caramels and ⅓ cup evaporated milk; set aside. Combine cake mix, butter, remaining ⅓ cup evaporated milk, and pecans. Press half of dough in greased 9x13-inch pan. Bake for 6 minutes. Remove from oven, and sprinkle with chocolate chips and caramel mixture. Crumble remaining dough over caramel layer. Bake for 15–18 minutes. Cool, then chill for at least 30 minutes before cutting.
Yield: 48 brownies

BUTTER PECAN SANDIES

1 (18-ounce) box butter pecan cake mix
1 (3¼-ounce) box vanilla instant pudding mix
1 egg
1 cup vegetable oil
1 cup chopped pecans

Preheat oven to 350 degrees. With mixer, combine cake mix, pudding mix, egg, and oil. Stir in pecans. Mold dough by pressing into a tablespoon, and place on a parchment-lined baking sheet. Bake for 12 minutes. Remove from oven and cool on wire rack.
Yield: 48 cookies

ICED SUGAR COOKIES

¾ cup shortening
1 cup sugar
2 eggs
1 teaspoon vanilla
2½ cups all-purpose flour
1 teaspoon baking powder
½ teaspoon salt

With mixer, cream shortening and sugar. Add eggs and vanilla; mix well. Combine dry ingredients; add to creamed mixture, mixing well. Divide dough in half; wrap in plastic wrap and chill for at least one hour. Preheat oven to 350 degrees. Roll half of dough to ¼-inch thickness on a lightly floured surface; keep remaining dough chilled. Cut dough into desired shapes with cookie cutters. Place on parchment-lined cookie sheets; bake 10 minutes, or until just starting to brown along bottom edges. Cool on a wire rack. Ice with Frosting.
Yield: 2 dozen cookies

FROSTING·

2½ cups confectioners' sugar, sifted
¼ cup hot water
1 teaspoon corn syrup
½ teaspoon vanilla

Stir ingredients together.

BUTTER COOKIE SPOONS

2 sticks unsalted butter, softened
1 cup sugar
1 egg
1 teaspoon vanilla
2½ cups all-purpose flour
¼ teaspoon salt
For garnish: lemon curd, fresh raspberries, and
    mint

With mixer, cream butter and sugar; add egg and vanilla. Combine flour and salt; gradually add to creamed mixture. Shape into 3 balls; place in large zipper bag; chill for 1 hour. Preheat oven to 375 degrees. Remove one ball at a time, roll to ¼-inch thickness on floured surface, and cut into spoon shapes with cutter. To personalize spoons, press a stamp letter on each handle. Bake 8–9 minutes or until lightly brown. Cool on wire rack. Just before serving, add ½ teaspoonful lemon curd, half of a raspberry, and a mint leaf to each spoon.
Yield: 4 dozen cookies

TOFFEE CRUNCH COOKIES

1½ cups all-purpose flour
½ teaspoon baking soda
½ teaspoon salt
1 stick butter
¾ cup packed brown sugar
1 egg
1 teaspoon vanilla
1 cup toffee bits
½ cup chopped pecans

Preheat oven to 350 degrees. Combine flour, soda, and salt. Cream butter and sugar. Add egg and vanilla; stir until creamy. Stir in dry ingredients. Blend in toffee bits and pecans. Drop by tablespoonfuls 2 inches apart on baking sheet. Bake for 10 minutes.
Yield: 24 cookies

CHERRY-ALMOND COOKIES

1 (17½-ounce) bag sugar cookie mix
1 stick butter, softened
1 egg
1 (12-ounce) package white chocolate chips
1 (6-ounce) package sweetened dried cherries
1 (6-ounce) package almonds, coarsely chopped

Preheat oven to 375 degrees. With mixer, combine cookie mix and butter. Add egg. Stir in chips, cherries, and nuts. Roll into 1-inch balls and place on ungreased cookie sheet. Bake for 8–10 minutes. Cool on a wire rack.
Yield: 24 cookies

SPECIAL CHOCOLATE CHIP COOKIES

1¼ cups all-purpose flour
1¼ teaspoons baking soda
½ teaspoon salt
½ cup shortening, softened
½ cup sugar
¼ cup packed brown sugar
1 tablespoon honey
1 egg, beaten
1 teaspoon vanilla
1 teaspoon Grand Marnier
1 cup semisweet chocolate chips

Preheat oven to 350 degrees. Combine flour, baking soda, and salt; set aside. With mixer, cream shortening, and sugars. Add honey, egg, vanilla, and Grand Marnier. Gradually blend in flour mixture. Stir in chips. Roll into walnut-size balls; press flat on parchment-lined baking sheet. Bake 8–10 minutes until golden. Cool on baking sheet for 2 minutes; remove to wire racks to cool completely.
Yield: 48 cookies

GINGERBREAD COOKIES

¾ cup shortening
1 cup brown sugar
¼ cup molasses
1 egg, beaten
2 cups all-purpose flour
½ teaspoon baking soda
⅛ teaspoon salt
½ teaspoon each: cloves and ginger
1 teaspoon cinnamon
1 (12-ounce) can vanilla frosting

Preheat oven to 375 degrees. Cream shortening, brown sugar, and molasses. Stir in egg. Combine dry ingredients and spices; add to shortening mixture. Roll to ¼ inch thick on floured surface, and cut into shapes with cookie cutter. Place on parchment-lined baking sheet, and sprinkle with sugar. Bake 8–10 minutes. Cool on wire rack. Pipe with icing and decorate with sprinkles and dragées.
Yield: 3–4 dozen cookies

PRALINE COOKIES

2 sticks unsalted butter, softened
1 cup packed dark brown sugar
1 egg
1 cup all-purpose flour
1 teaspoon vanilla
1 cup chopped pecans

Preheat oven to 350 degrees. Cream butter and sugar. Stir in egg. Add flour and vanilla. Fold in pecans. Drop by tablespoonfuls on parchment-lined baking sheets. Bake 13–15 minutes. Cool on baking sheets 1 minute before removing to wire rack.
Yield: 2 dozen cookies

Gingerbread Cookies

Chocolate Nut Clusters and Microwave Pralines

CHOCOLATE NUT CLUSTERS

1 (24-ounce) package chocolate almond bark
1 (12-ounce) package semisweet chocolate chips
1 (24-ounce) can salted peanuts

In microwave, on DEFROST, heat almond bark and chips at 2-minute intervals until melted. Stir in peanuts, and spoon onto wax paper in small mounds.
Yield: 36 clusters

CHOCOLATE-COVERED MARSHMALLOWS AND PECANS

1 (24-ounce) package chocolate almond bark
1 (12-ounce) package semisweet chocolate chips
1 cup pecan halves
1 cup mini marshmallows

In microwave, on DEFROST, heat almond bark and chips at 2-minute intervals until melted. Cool slightly. Stir in pecans and marshmallows. Spoon onto wax paper in small mounds.
Yield: 36 pieces

TURTLES

72 pecan halves
24 caramels, unwrapped
6 ounces chocolate almond bark
1 (6-ounce) package semisweet chocolate chips

Preheat oven to 300 degrees. On a greased baking sheet, arrange pecan halves in groups of three, end to end, flat sides down. Place a caramel on top of each cluster of pecans. Place in oven for 5 minutes until caramels soften. Remove from oven and flatten each caramel with a buttered spoon. Cool slightly. In microwave, on DEFROST, heat almond bark and chips at 2-minute intervals until melted. Dip turtles in chocolate to coat; place on wax paper.
Yield: 24 turtles

SEA SALT CARAMELS

This is the easiest recipe for homemade candy!

1 (14-ounce) bag caramels, unwrapped
1 (24-ounce) package chocolate almond bark
1 (12-ounce) package semisweet chocolate chips
1 tablespoon coarse sea salt

Slightly flatten caramels with palm of hand; set aside. In microwave, on DEFROST, heat almond bark and chips at 2-minute intervals until melted. Dip caramels in melted chocolate and drop onto wax paper. Sprinkle with sea salt.
Yield: 48 pieces

WHITE CHOCOLATE-CHERRY DROPS

1 (24-ounce) package vanilla almond bark
²⁄₃ cup slivered almonds
1 teaspoon almond extract
1 (12-ounce) jar maraschino cherries, drained and chopped

In microwave on DEFROST, heat bark at 1-minute intervals until melted. Add almonds, extract, and cherries; stir well. Pour on wax paper, spreading until mixture is ¼ inch thick. Cool, and break into pieces.
Yield: 60 pieces

MICROWAVE PRALINES

½ pint whipping cream
1 pound light brown sugar
2 tablespoons margarine
2 cups pecan halves

Microwave whipping cream and brown sugar on HIGH for 13 minutes. Stir in margarine and pecans. Stir until not shiny. Drop onto foil.
Yield: 24 pieces

CRACKER CANDY

2 sleeves saltine crackers
2 sticks butter
1 cup brown sugar
8 ounces semisweet chocolate chips

Preheat oven to 400 degrees. Line a 9x13-inch jellyroll pan with foil, and place saltines over entire pan. Over medium heat, bring butter and brown sugar to a boil for 3 minutes or until frothy. Remove from heat and pour over crackers. Bake for 5 minutes. Remove from oven and sprinkle with chocolate chips. Return to oven for 5 minutes. Remove from oven and let sit for 5 minutes. Using a metal spatula, spread chocolate over crackers. Chill in pan for 1 hour. Remove from refrigerator and break into pieces. Store in an airtight container.
Yield: 1 pound candy

NUTTY CLUB CRACKERS

2 sleeves club crackers
1 stick butter
1 stick margarine
½ cup sugar
1 cup chopped pecans
1 teaspoon vanilla

Preheat oven to 300 degrees. Spread crackers on greased, foil-lined baking sheet with edges. In saucepan, heat butter, margarine, and sugar to a boil for 3 minutes. Stir in pecans and vanilla. Pour sugar mixture over crackers and bake for 8–10 minutes.
Yield: 36 crackers

MICROWAVE ENGLISH TOFFEE

¾ cup chopped almonds, divided
1 stick butter
1 cup sugar
1 teaspoon salt
¼ cup water
3 (41-gram) Hershey's chocolate bars with almonds, broken

Sprinkle ½ cup almonds on greased, foil-lined baking sheet with sides. Coat bottom and side of a 2-quart glass bowl with butter. Add butter, sugar, salt, and water. Microwave for 11 minutes on HIGH. Pour hot mixture over almonds on baking sheet. Sprinkle with chocolate pieces. Let stand for 2 minutes; spread chocolate, and sprinkle with remaining almonds. Cool, and break into bite-size pieces.
Yield: about 36 pieces

CARAMELS

1 (14-ounce) can sweetened condensed milk
1 cup light corn syrup
2½ cups packed light brown sugar
2 sticks butter, softened
⅛ teaspoon salt
1 tablespoon vanilla
¾ cup finely chopped pecans

In a 2-quart glass bowl, combine condensed milk, corn syrup, brown sugar, butter, and salt. Microwave on HIGH for 4 minutes, or until butter is melted. Stir until mixture is blended. Microwave on HIGH for 14 minutes or until mixture reaches 245 degrees (firm-ball stage) on candy thermometer. Add vanilla and pecans; mix well. Let stand 10 minutes. Pour into a greased, foil-lined 9x13-inch pan. Chill. Place candy slab on cutting board; cut into 1-inch squares. Wrap each piece in wax paper, twisting ends, or in plastic wrap, folding ends under.
Yield: about 100 pieces

FUDGE

1½ sticks butter
3 cups sugar
1 (5-ounce) can evaporated milk
1 (12-ounce) bag semisweet chocolate chips
1 (7-ounce) jar marshmallow crème
¾ cup chopped pecans
1 teaspoon vanilla
For garnish: fondant flowers

In saucepan over medium heat, combine butter, sugar, and milk. Heat 4 minutes. After bubbles appear, heat 3 minutes. When it reaches soft-ball stage, remove from heat. Stir in chips and marshmallow crème. Stir in pecans and vanilla. Continue stirring until thick. Pour into 9x13-inch dish lined with greased wax paper. Cool, and cut into pieces. Garnish with fondant flowers and dragées.
Yield: 36 pieces

MICROWAVE DIVINITY

4 cups sugar
1 cup light corn syrup
¾ cup water
⅛ teaspoon salt
3 egg whites
1½ cups chopped pecans
1½ teaspoons vanilla

Microwave sugar, corn syrup, water, and salt for 19 minutes on HIGH, stirring every 5 minutes. With mixer, beat egg whites for 19 minutes while sugar mixture is cooking. Gradually pour hot syrup into egg whites. Continue beating on high until thick and not glossy, about 10 minutes. Stir in pecans and vanilla. Drop by teaspoonfuls onto wax paper.
Yield: about 36 pieces

Fudge

CAKE TRUFFLES

2 medium slices each: Italian cream cake, strawberry cake, German chocolate cake
6–8 ounces vanilla almond bark
6–8 ounces chocolate almond bark
For garnish: sprinkles, grated coconut, and finely chopped pecans

With mixer, beat 2 slices of one kind of cake at a time (including icing) until combined. Shape into 1-inch balls and freeze on wax paper for 2 hours. In microwave on DEFROST, melt candy coating 4–6 ounces at a time at 1-minute intervals until melted. Dip Italian cream cake truffles into melted vanilla almond bark, and sprinkle with chopped pecans. Dip strawberry cake truffles into melted vanilla almond bark with a few drops of red food coloring, and decorate with sprinkles or coconut. Dip German chocolate cake truffles into melted chocolate almond bark, and sprinkle with chocolate sprinkles. Drop on wax paper.
Yield: 10–12 truffles per 2 slices of cake

PEANUT BUTTER TRUFFLES

1 (16-ounce) box confectioners' sugar
1 (12-ounce) jar crunchy peanut butter
1½ sticks butter, softened
1 (24-ounce) package chocolate almond bark, melted

With hands, combine sugar, peanut butter, and butter. Roll into walnut-sized balls, place on wax paper-lined cookie sheet, and chill overnight. Dip in almond bark, and place on wax paper to harden.
Yield: about 100 pieces

ORANGE PECAN TRUFFLES

1 (12-ounce) package vanilla wafers, crushed
1½ cups confectioners' sugar, divided
½ stick butter, softened
1 (6-ounce) can frozen orange juice concentrate, thawed
1 teaspoon vanilla
1¼ cups chopped pecans

Combine crumbs and 1 cup sugar; mix with butter and orange juice concentrate; add vanilla and nuts. Shape into small balls; shake in bag with remaining ½ cup confectioners' sugar. Arrange orange balls in single layer on tray; store uncovered overnight in refrigerator.
Yield: 40–50 balls

CREAM CHEESE MINTS

1 (3-ounce) package cream cheese, softened
2½ cups confectioners' sugar
3 drops peppermint flavoring
Food coloring (optional)
Sugar

With mixer, combine cream cheese and confectioners' sugar. Add flavoring and coloring, if desired. Roll into small balls; roll balls in sugar. Press into mold. Remove from mold; chill until serving.
Yield: 40 pieces

CREDITS

PHOTOGRAPHERS

Tom Beck

22, 76, 85, 197

Ron Blaylock

Front cover, author (back cover and 224), 6, 39, 40, 47, 54, 57, 65, 77, 81, 94, 95, 102, 122, 125, 130, 131, 135, 147, 153, 190

Greg Campbell

Back cover (center and right), 10, 12, 13, 14, 24, 26, 36, 43, 49, 52, 58, 60, 62, 63, 66, 72, 74, 79, 90, 97, 105, 106, 108, 112, 115, 116, 119, 121, 126, 129, 132, 136, 142, 151, 158, 171, 175, 185, 186, 189, 192, 193, 194, 198, 203, 204, 207, 208, 211, 213

Bonnie Dickerson

Back cover (left), 2, 4, 17, 18, 21, 28, 29, 30, 33, 34, 35, 44, 46, 48, 50, 69, 70, 73, 75, 82, 86, 89, 93, 98, 101, 103, 111, 128, 139, 141, 144, 148, 154, 157, 161, 162, 164, 167, 168, 176, 178, 181, 183, 195, 200, 214, 217

Tempy Segrest

8, 172

HOMES AND SETTINGS

Kelly and Dean Andrews 122

The Late Mike Corso 43

Pat Cothren and Jim Wilkirson 81

Kathyrn and Keith Davis 10, 13, 14

Kathleen and Jim Foshee 36, 90

Carolyn and Ben Hodges 58, 115, 186

Becky and Herb Ivison 85

Trey Massy 125

Charlotte and Curtis McKee 26

Glenda and Danny Robinson 30, 195

Melanie and Locke Ward 40, 116

RECIPE CREDITS

Kaci Allen

Kelly Andrews

Sharon Armstrong

Rita Black

Mary Alice Blackmon

Cynthia B. Blackwell

Candy Blue

Toliver Bozeman, III

Charlene Bullock

Michael Bullock

Amy Bowling

Selina Boyles

Emily Burgess

Wyonda Cain

Suellen Calhoun

Pat Caskey

Lena Causey

Kay Ciarletta

Pat Clark

Gail Collins

Ann Conner

Judy Davis

Kathryn Davis

Sheila Day

Joni Duperior

Janice Durden

Jean Easterling

Joan B. Ferguson

Peggy Foggin

Greg Fontenot

Shea Fox

Billie Jean Giffin

Shirley A. Glaab

Pam Glover

Jeff Good

Merry Graham

Lisa Grantham

Tamra L. Grimes

Joey Halinski

Gale Hammond

Jeff Hammond

Kelley Hansbrough

Karis Harbarger

Carol Hardison

Willard Harrell

Melinda Hart

Buddy Hatchell

Taylor Hawks

Drew Hayslett

Carolyn Heidelberg

Kathy Helstrom

Rosie Henderson

Anna Henson

Meg Henson

Clara Higgenbotham

Sara Highfill

Madalyn Hindman

Carolyn Hodges

Ben Hodges

Linda Hogue

Susan Horn

Katy Houston

Jim Hudson

Debbie Huston

Winnifred Jackson

Paula McTune Jones

Lucy Hollis Jones

Charlotte Kidd

Rebecca Laney-Meers

Joan P. Lansdell

Mary Ellen Lawrence

Natalie Baker Lindell

Susan Lott

Nicole Luciano-Epperson

Pat Lyon

Trey Massey

Mary Jane McDaniel

Sara McDaniel

Johnnie McKinnon

Georgia Miller

Emily Mitchell

Patty Mitchell

Mary Jane Moak

Sheila Moore

Mary Frances Mullen

Sarah Murphy

Bill Naids

Brittany Odom

Gray Ouzts

Martha Partridge

Elizabeth Pegg

Jann W. Puckett

Sandra Rainer

Jane Richardson

Glenda Robinson

Melanie Roper

Penny Roper

Michaela Rosenthal

Tempy Segrest

Laura Shirley

Peggy Shivers

Cheryl Sides

Pam Simpson

Evelyn Slay

June Smith

Kay Smith

Ruth Smith

Kim Snellings

Kathy Snyder

Angela Spengler

Susan Spicer

Judith Stechmann

Sue Ann Stewart

Pat Stockett

Gayla Stone

Melanie Taylor

Arlette Thompson

Bonnie Tigrett

Grace Toler

Charla Walker

Laurie Walker

Carole Ward

Melanie Ward

Kim Waters

Jeanie Watkins

Jamie Werne

Carmen Wolfe

Beth Young

Dorthy Young

INDEX

ABOUT THE AUTHOR

A native Mississippian, Patty Roper received her bachelor of arts degree from the University of Mississippi and taught elementary school in Mississippi for ten years. She is a member of First Presbyterian Church, Jackson, Mississippi, where she has served on various committees. She has held many positions with the Symphony League, garden clubs, Bible studies, schools, and other volunteer organizations.

Patty entertains family and friends with a classic, practical approach to beauty with fresh ideas, attention to details, and innovative ways to save time, effort, and expense. She is the editorial director of *Mississippi Magazine* and shares entertaining and decorating ideas in the "Easy Does It" department. She is the author of *Easy Hospitality, Easy Does It Entertaining, At the Table with Patty Roper,* and *Easy Parties and Wedding Celebrations*. She and her husband Richard live in Flowood, Mississippi, and have one daughter Beth.